THE PREPARATION OF MONETARY POLICY

The Preparation of Monetary Policy

Essays on a Multi-Model Approach

by

Jan Marc Berk
De Nederlandsche Bank, Amsterdam,
Free University, Amsterdam

KLUWER ACADEMIC PUBLISHERS
BOSTON / DORDRECHT / LONDON

A C.I.P. Catalogue record for this book is available from the Library of Congress.

ISBN 0-7923-7269-7

Published by Kluwer Academic Publishers,
P.O. Box 17, 3300 AA Dordrecht, The Netherlands.

Sold and distributed in North, Central and South America
by Kluwer Academic Publishers,
101 Philip Drive, Norwell, MA 02061, U.S.A.

In all other countries, sold and distributed
by Kluwer Academic Publishers,
P.O. Box 322, 3300 AH Dordrecht, The Netherlands.

Printed on acid-free paper

Printed in the Netherlands.

CONTENTS

Acknowledgements vii

1 Introduction and Overview

1. Outline of the chapter 1
2. Monetary policy - some conceptual issues 2
3. The monetary transmission mechanism 7
4. Implications for the foundations of monetary policy: a multi-model approach 14
5. Topics studied 20

2 The Information Content of the Yield Curve for Monetary Policy: a Survey

1. Introduction 23
2. Theories of the yield curve 25
   2.1 Yield curve and future inflation rates 25
   2.2 Yield curve and future economic activity 27
3. The empirical validity of different theories 29
   3.1 The information content with respect to future inflation 29
   3.2 The information content with respect to future economic activity 32
4. Implications for monetary policy 33
5. Concluding remarks 36

3 Co-Movements in Long-Term Interest Rates and the Role of Exchange Rate Expectations: Evidence from Survey Data

1. Introduction 39
2. Recent developments in international bond markets: a first look 40
3. Survey data and methodology 46
4. Empirical results 52
5. Concluding remarks 57

4 International Interdependence of Business Cycles: The Use of Leading Indicators for Forecasting and Analysis

1.	Introduction	59
2.	Measuring business cycles	60
3.	Constructing a composite leading indicator	63
4.	Selection of basic indicators and countries	65
5.	Empirical results	67
6.	International interdependence of business cycles	76
7.	National indicators with an international component	79
8.	Concluding remarks	81

5 Measuring Inflation Expectations: a Survey Data Approach

1.	Introduction	87
2.	On the estimation of inflationary expectations from qualitative responses	88
2.1	The distribution of inflation expectations	89
2.2	The perceived inflation rate	92
3.	Empirical analysis	93
4.	The usefulness of directly estimated expected inflation measures for monetary policy	100
5.	Concluding remarks	102
Appendix		103

6 Price Movements in the Netherlands and Germany and the Guilder-Dmark Peg

1.	Introduction	109
2.	Theoretical framework	109
3.	Empirical results	113
4.	Concluding remarks	119
Appendix		120

7 Summary and Concluding Remarks

1.	Summary	121
2.	Concluding remarks	124

References 127

Index 147

Acknowledgements

This study is the result of research conducted over the past few years at the Domestic Research Department and its successor, the Monetary and Economic Policy Department, of the Nederlandsche Bank (DNB). DNB gave me the opportunity to work on the project, and my collegues provided a stimulative and, by their congenial cooperation, productive research atmosphere. Without meaning to detract from the help of others, special thanks go to Job Swank, Lex Hoogduin and Elmer Sterken for their encouragement, enthusiasm, and unconditional support. They provided numerous useful suggestions, and took the time and patience to bear with me in many stimulating discussions. I would furthermore like to thank my collegues Jaap Bikker, Klaas Knot, and Carlo Winder for their kind permission to use the papers I co-authored with them in this study. Thanks are also due to Aerdt Houben for his willingness to read the entire manuscript and to provide me with useful comments. Henk van Kerkhoff provided expert research assistance, and Bibian Verkade and Rodetta Noordwijk skillfully typed some tedious parts of the manuscript. I wish to thank them all. Finally, I would like to thank the editors of *Applied Economics*, *De Economist* and *Journal of Forecasting* for their permission to let me use articles that have been published in their journals.

This book would never have been written without the backing of the homefront. In this respect, I owe a debt of gratitude to Bianca, and apologies to Brian and Ian, for my frequent mental and sometimes physical absence during this project.

1 INTRODUCTION AND OVERVIEW

1.1 Outline of the chapter

For a central bank to achieve its ultimate objective(s), it would be preferable to know in detail how monetary policy affects non-financial activity, that is inflation and real output. In practice, however, the central bank only has imperfect knowledge of the exact interactions that take place within various chains of the monetary transmission mechanism, but has (subjective) probability distributions in mind. The leitmotiv of this book is that this uncertainty should have implications for the preparation of monetary policy. Our goal is to translate the intricate interactions between various endogenous and exogenous variables (policy instruments) into simple relationships. These could then serve as guidelines for and legitimation of specific forms of monetary policy. Or, to put it differently, the degree of transparency of monetary policy and the successful use of rules in conducting monetary policy may be said to, *inter alia*, depend on the ability of the central bank to establish such relationships empirically. We study some of these relationships in subsequent chapters. The purpose of this chapter is to clarify some important theoretical concepts in order to illustrate the interrelationships between the following chapters.

The next section contains a general description of important concepts used in the formulation of monetary policy. This provides us with the necessary tools to discuss in more detail the various channels through which monetary policy decisions affect policy targets in section 3. It is concluded from this section that there exists considerable ambiguity regarding the various transmission channels actually operating in the economy. Economic theory provides us with some basic notions, but the transmission mechanism in practice is determined by structural, behavioural and institutional factors. Given this uncertainty, a general framework for preparing a strategy of monetary policy is proposed, in section 4. Our hypothesis is that, since the transmission mechanism is too complex to be adequately described by a single large structural model designed to answer all questions, the policy maker should also rely on a complementary range of models, dealing with specific chains in the transmission mechanism. This provides him flexibility in addressing specific questions and in allowing new information to be processed and evaluated in a relatively short span of time. The subsequent chapters of this book contain illustrations or case studies of this approach; the choice of subjects is motivated in section 5.

1.2 Monetary policy - some conceptual issues

Final objectives of economic policy are stated in terms of variables deemed to influence directly the welfare of individuals and society. We denote the latter variables as *ultimate-target variables*; they are pursued in their own right as final goals of economic policy. The volume of output, aggregate employment and the price level are often regarded as ultimate target variables. Stability of the price level is naturally associated with monetary policy, since it is generally accepted that inflation in the long run is a monetary phenomenon. In recent years, this fairly general statement has been sharpened considerably, to the extent that monetary authorities throughout the world are now moving to adopt medium- to long-run price stability as their primary goal (Kahn, 1996). The latter statement needs some clarification.[1] First, the fundamental reason to pursue price stability is that inflation is economically and socially costly. This hypothesis is by now fairly well documented (see, for example, Barro, 1995; Fischer, 1981, 1994; Fischer and Modigliani, 1978), and will not be discussed here. The costs of inflation depend on the institutional structure of the economy, in particular the tax system and especially the taxation of capital, and on the extent to which the inflation rate has been anticipated.[2] Second, the primary reason for making price stability the goal of monetary policy as conducted by an independent central bank is the inflationary bias inherent in monetary policy (Cukierman, 1992; Walsh, 1993; Debelle and Fischer, 1994; Fuhrer, 1997). This notion has its roots in the 'time inconsistency' literature, as developed by Kydland and Prescott (1977) and Barro and Gordon (1983). The thrust of this argument is that monetary policy makers who pursue price stability as well as employment growth could end up with a higher inflation outcome, with no better employment outcome, than one that is solely focussed on price stability (Sijben, 1992). Third, in stating, as we do, that price stability should be the final objective of monetary policy, it is important to be clear about what is meant by price stability, as it can have different interpretations with different implications.

Defining price stability

Monetary policy could target a constant price level, a zero inflation rate, an upward drifting price level or a low but nonzero rate of inflation (Bernanke and Mishkin, 1997; Fischer, 1994, 1996; Goodhart and Viñals, 1994). An advantage of a price level target is that it keeps uncertainty about price levels

---

[1] Goodhart and Viñals (1994); Okina (1995); Fuhrer (1997).

[2] See Feldstein (1996) for a calculation of the economic costs of inflation in the US implied by the interaction of the tax system and inflation.

in the distant future smaller than it would be with a zero inflation target, which entails base drift. The chief disadvantage is that it puts greater strains on monetary policy, because variations in the inflation rate are required to reverse the effects of previous shocks on the price level. There are in addition several reasons for aiming for a small positive inflation rate in stead of a zero rate. First, the true rate of inflation is below the measured rate, due to measurement problems (Debelle, 1997). Second, as Akerlof, Dickens and Perry (1996) point out, if nominal wages are rigid downward, then reductions in real wages will involve less employment loss when brought about through inflation. Very low inflation therefore effectively reduces real-wage flexibility and may worsen the allocative efficiency of the labour market.[3] Third, with a zero targeted inflation rate, there is a greater chance of deflation. As pointed out in the literature on financial crises, persistent deflation can create serious problems for the financial system (Fisher, 1933; Bernanke and James, 1991; Mishkin, 1991). Fourth, the lower bound of zero on the nominal interest rate that arises because cash carries a zero nominal interest rate imposes problems for monetary policy with a zero targeted inflation rate (Summers, 1991). If the expected inflation rate is zero, it is very difficult to engineer a negative short-run real interest rate (which may be needed during recessions). These arguments lead us to conclude that price stability is best interpreted as achieving and maintaining a low and stable rate of inflation. Correspondingly, in this book, we define the inflation rate as the ultimate target variable for monetary policy, which is in line with the actual practice followed by most if not all central banks.

Acknowledging that a low level of inflation should be the central goal of monetary policy, however, does not imply that monetary policy should ignore output movements.[4] Although it is widely, though not universally, accepted that there is no permanent trade-off between price stability and economic growth[5], this does not apply in quite the same way to the short run (Papademos and Modigliani, 1990; Brunner and Meltzer, 1976). Econometric studies in the US and elsewhere establish the existence of a short-run trade-off between inflation and growth (Gordon, 1990; Romer,

---

[3] In contrast, price level stability is a device to stabilise economies with coordination failures. More specifically, downward wage rigidity provides a break against runaway deflation. It is thus a feature of labour markets that stabilise the economy against extreme outcomes by reducing deflationary expectations and permitting real interest rates to fall (Akerlof, Dickens and Perry, 1996, pp. 51/52).

[4] See Romer and Romer (1996) for a discussion of the institutional settings of the central bank most conducive to realising monetary stability.

[5] Fair (1996), working with data from thirty countries, finds that functional forms for price and wage equations that imply the possibility of a long-run Phillips curve tradeoff on the whole perform better than those implying no tradeoff. For recent research on the contrary, see Bullard and Keating (1995).

1996).[6] When an economy is hit by an inflationary shock, for example, the decision on how quickly to return to the trend rate of price increase does have implications for the level of output in the transition period. The implication is that the monetary authority is also interested in the effects its policy decisions elicit in the short term on real economic activity. This motivates the frequent use in this book of the concept of non-financial activity, which comprises inflation as well as real output.

Monetary policy makers have at their disposal certain *operational targets* of economic policy; i.e. variables that are directly under the control of the monetary authorities, who have some discretion regarding the selection of particular variables to use as operational targets. The monetary authority faces a basic choice between selecting a 'price' or a 'quantity' as its primary operational target. In particular, it can choose either a short-run market interest rate (such as the overnight rate, i.e. the rate at which commercial banks lend immediately available funds to each other), or the amount of a central bank liability (such as base money). Both variables are potential operational targets.[7] None of them is directly related to economic welfare. The purpose of controlling them is simply to influence other variables which are more directly related to welfare. To achieve these operational targets, central banks have at their disposition certain sets of *instruments*, especially reserve requirements, standing facilities and open market operations. In most countries the actual instrument is the change in the central bank balance sheet that results in the desired change in a very short-term market interest rate. The latter functions as an operational target. This target could be the overnight rate, but also 1 to 3 months interest rates. Below we will use the label instrument in a rather broad sense, pertaining to the operational target as well as the actual instruments available to achieve these targets.

Intermediate variables are like operational targets in the sense that they have no direct significance for social and economic welfare; their main importance (and the reason why the monetary authority may attempt to target

---

[6] Early theoretical explanations of the existence of a short-run Phillips curve include expectational errors (assuming adaptive expectations; Phelps,1967; Friedman, 1968). Under rational expectations, Lucas (1973) argued that a short-run trade-off between inflation and output was the result of signal processing errors of economic agents (confusion by buyers and sellers about the meaning of changes in nominal prices). It could not be exploited for policy purposes. In contrast to this new classical approach, other explanations argue that monetary policy influences real activity because of the existence of sticky wages and prices. Recent research has produced models that explain these nominal rigidities as the outcome of optimizing behaviour, see Ball, Mankiw and Romer (1988); Mankiw and Romer (1991). This line of inquiry also provides evidence that the curvature of the Phillips curve depends on the level of inflation rates (Fischer,1996; Akerlof, Dickens and Perry,1996).

[7] Once one of the two is selected as the primary actual operational target, the other cannot be controlled precisely. Only in a non-stochastic system is the setting of price variables the dual of fixing quantities and vice versa (Papademos and Modigliani, 1990; Bryant, Hooper and Mann, 1993).

these variables) lies in the alleged relationship with the ultimate target variable. The main difference between operational and intermediate variables is that while the former are narrowly controlled by the policy maker, the latter can not generally be influenced with great precision. This is because intermediate variables are determined by the behaviour of private sector agents as well as of policy makers. The question then naturally arises as to why the policy maker should target an intermediate variable instead of directly focussing on realising the ultimate target.[8] In other words, why transform the making of monetary policy into a two-stage procedure? In the first stage of this procedure policy makers determine the value of the intermediate target chosen that would be consistent with achieving their ultimate target.[9] In the second stage the central bank acts to achieve this projected value of the intermediate target.[10] This two-stage procedure is a reaction to the dynamic and stochastic environment in which the policy maker operates. As elaborated by, e.g., B. Friedman (1990, 1996), Groeneveld et al. (1996) and Sijben (1977), the fact that policy actions and their economic effects are separated both by time and by behavioural process (see sections 3 and 4) implies that grounding monetary policy on intermediate targets provides a coherent way of taking the consequences of (unavoidable) unexpected developments into account. A second argument for a role for intermediate targets is in using them as signals to the public about monetary policy intentions and thus as instruments to influence inflation expectations (Bernanke and Mishkin, 1992; Poole, 1994).

A final class of variables is the *indicator, or information, variables* (Burger, 1971; B. Friedman, 1990). They can be defined as having information value regarding the impact of operational targets on the outcomes of ultimate target variables, but are not themselves an object of control (as was the case for intermediate variables). Indicator variables can include variables that, in another context, may be viewed as an intermediate target. For example, the growth rate of the money stock can be viewed as an intermediate target, but it can also be seen as an indicator of the potential strength of actual demand in the economy. Other indicator variables are those that convey information about the future evolution of the economy. They include, among other things, variables relating to the current and future level of real economic activity (leading and coincident indicators) and

[8] There exists a lively and as yet unresolved debate about the advisability of targeting intermediate variables, see for example M. Friedman (1959, 1968, 1982); Kareken, Muench and Wallace (1973); Waud (1973); B. Friedman (1975, 1977, 1990, 1993, 1994); Bryant (1980, 1983); McCallum (1985, 1990).

[9] Thereby implictly assuming that the choice of intermediate target is already made. This choice will be discussed shortly.

[10] In the second stage of this procedure, the policy maker aligns his operational target to the desired outcome of the intermediate target. This is realised with the instruments the central bank has at its disposition.

expectational indices, including expectations derived from financial variables and from surveys. Some of the chapters of this book are devoted to the analysis of various indicator variables.

The task facing policy makers is then to choose particular intermediate targets and information variables and to develop procedures for intertemporal variation of these targets such that the economy is most likely to attain the best feasible combination of time paths for the ultimate-target variable. The way in which policy makers resolve the issues of choice and variation of intermediate targets constitutes the *monetary strategy*. The monetary strategy followed manifests itself in *monetary policy* decisions, i.e. decisions concerning the choice of and intertemporal variation in operational targets such as to achieve the projected outcome for the intermediate target variable.

Regarding the choice of intermediate target, a voluminous literature developed.[11] It becomes apparent from this literature that the optimal choice depends in part on the nature of disturbances influencing the economy. In actual practice, central banks target monetary aggregates (for example, the Bundesbank prior to the start of stage three of EMU), the exchange rate (De Nederlandsche Bank until January 1999), or expected inflation (Bank of England). In addition, the Federal Reserve does not target intermediate variables, but instead uses an eclectic strategy (Feldstein and Stock, 1994). In the latter strategy, a variety of information variables is used for monetary policy purposes, with different weights placed on different variables depending on the particular circumstances. For a recent discussion of intermediate monetary targeting, see Estrella and Mishkin (1996) and Poole (1994). The experience in the Netherlands with intermediate targeting of the exchange rate is discussed in a subsequent chapter of this book. The same applies to the use of expected inflation as an intermediate target, which is the central tenet of the so-called 'direct' (an unfortunate terminology) inflation targeting strategy (Svensson, 1996; Green, 1996; Bernanke and Mishkin, 1997).[12] See Ball (1997) for an evaluation of various monetary policy rules.

A monetary strategy is thus the foremost important element of any monetary policy. But a prerequisite for a successful monetary strategy is an understanding of the relationship between operational targets and ultimate target variables (Romer and Romer, 1996). A shorthand commonly used to describe the complex chains of behavioural causation between these two

---

[11] See Papademos and Modigliani (1990) and Bryant, Hooper and Mann (1993) for a theoretical discussion and an empirical evaluation, respectively. See also the study by the European Monetary Institute regarding the monetary policy strategy of the ESCB (EMI, 1997).

[12] In an inflation-targeting strategy, the monetary policymaker announces a target or a target range for future inflation. A change in the current policy stance is indicated if projected inflation over a medium-term horizon falls outside the announced range. Thus, in contrast to its name, direct inflation targeting is in fact an intermediate targeting procedure (Svensson, 1996).

types of variables is that of the *monetary transmission mechanism*. This mechanism can be seen as a dynamic process through which monetary policy decisions (i.e. the deployment of instrument variables) are transmitted into the ultimate policy objective (Taylor, 1995). There are many different views of the monetary transmission mechanism. These views differ in the emphasis they place on money, credit, interest rates, exchange rates, asset prices or the role of commercial banks and other financial institutions. Given the primary objective of this book - to present an analysis of interactions that take place in different chains of the monetary transmission mechanism - it is clear that we must discuss this mechanism in more detail.

1.3 The monetary transmission mechanism

A description of the various channels through which monetary policy decisions may affect the ultimate policy target, that is, the monetary transmission mechanism, is useful for several reasons. The most obvious is that such knowledge is important for a successful conduct of monetary policy (M. Friedman, 1969; Sijben, 1977). Moreover, the transmission mechanism describes how private-sector agents respond to the policy actions of the monetary authorities, and how the monetary authorities and the private sector then interact. Important factors conditioning the behaviour of economic agents (and the policy maker, for that matter) are institutional and structural factors, in particular those determining the functioning of markets, the financial behaviour of firms and financial intermediaries and the composition of their balance sheets (Mankiw and Romer, 1991; BIS, 1995). These factors are not constant, but subject to ongoing change. Moreover, economic agents operate in an uncertain environment, so that their decisions are based on expectations regarding factors relevant for those decisions, such as the behaviour of the monetary policy maker.[13] The strategy followed by the monetary policymaker must take these kind of changes and expectations into account. The fact that the monetary authority interacts with a changing environment implies that the chains of the monetary transmission mechanism actually form a circle, with the circle being closed by linking the movements in the ultimate target variable back to the instrument variable through a policy rule or reaction function (Taylor, 1995, 1996). Knowledge of the transmission process can thus have an important bearing on the monetary strategy (Mishkin, 1996). More specifically, if the outcome with respect to the ultimate target variable differs from that which the monetary policy authority had projected, there might have to be a revision of the strategy (Freedman, 1996).[14] It is therefore useful to discuss this transmission process

[13] For a discussion of uncertainty in a monetary economy, see Hoogduin (1991).
[14] Of course, revision of the strategy is not the first action to be taken by the policy maker.

in more detail.

There exist different views of the monetary transmission mechanism (see Mishkin, 1995, for an overview). It consists of several channels, all of them interlinked and each of them comprising of several stages. Central to these different views are alternative conceptions regarding the structural and institutional factors mentioned above, more specifically the functioning of credit, labour and product markets. To illustrate the working of the monetary transmission mechanism and the role of these factors, we consider it useful, for presentational purposes, to highlight the following elements:[15]

1. the influence of changes in the instrument variables on the cost of finance;
2. the influence of changes in the cost of finance on expenditure decisions of private-sector agents, i.e. on non-financial activity;
3. the passthrough of changes in non-financial activity to output and inflation (in particular the split between real activity and inflation).

Before discussing these elements in more detail, we make three observations. First, underlying this division of the transmission mechanism into separate stages, is the conception that markets do not necessarily clear instantaneously. If, on the other hand, markets did always clear, a change in the instrument variable would immediately lead to a compensating change in the price level, without having consequences for output, and maintaining the classical dichotomy. Second, in addition to the nominal rigidites just mentioned, we explictly allow for the possibility of real rigidities, by exploring the relations between a change in the instrument variable of monetary policy and non-financial activity under credit market imperfections. The latter are a result of asymmetric information between lenders and borrowers (Stiglitz and Weiss, 1981; Bernanke, 1983; Bernanke and Blinder, 1988). To position these observations in macroeconomic theory, new classical or real business cycle theory would reject both kinds of rigidities, 'traditional' Keynesian economic theory would accept nominal but does not mention real rigidities, and new Keynesian economics would accept both nominal and real rigidities (Mankiw and Romer, 1991). Third, it is more or less generally accepted that changes in the instrument variable in the long run only affects prices, so that money is neutral in the long run (see the second section). Possible short run barriers to full and immediate nominal adjustment ('nominal' rigidities) are not inconsistent with this view. Whether the same applies to situations in which supply and demand do not come together because of market failures ('real rigidities'), is not clear. The

---

Confronted with persistent differences between projections and actual outcomes, the policy maker will first change his policy instruments. If this is not succesful in aligning projection and outcome, revision of stategy becomes an option.

[15] The transmission mechanism is a dynamic process, in that it represents a sequence of events taking place at successive moments in time. The ordering below reflects the timing of this sequence.

literature on credit market imperfections, for example, does not address this issue, because of the basically static nature of the analysis.[16] Usually it is (implicitly) assumed that these real rigidities are not long-run phenomena, implying long-run money neutrality.

Examining the first stage

The presumption underlying this element is that the monetary authority exercises power over economic behaviour of private-sector agents by influencing the financial (opportunity) cost relevant for the spending decisions of these agents. The typical operational target used by central banks is the overnight rate, which the central bank broadly determines through its influence on bank reserves (Crockett, 1994). According to BIS (1994), the passthrough from these overnight rates to short-term market interest rates is fairly complete in most industrialised countries. We take this to imply that the central bank can, for all intents and purposes, control the short-term market interest rate (see also Wellink, 1990; Bernanke and Blinder, 1992; Mauskopf, 1990; Blinder, 1997). However, the level of short-term market interest rates affects only a proportion of the financing of expenditure of households and firms. The private sector also finances part of its spending at longer-term rates on the capital market as well as through financial intermediaries (and through other means like retentions and equity issues), and the cost of borrowing from these sources is only indirectly influenced by the current level of money market rates. Important determinants of the impact of changes in the instrument variable (the overnight rate) on the cost of finance thus include:

- the substitutability between different forms of finance;
- the passthrough of changes in market interest rates to bank lending and deposit rates;
- the impact of changes in short-term interest rates on long-term interest rates.

The substitutability between different forms of finance and the responses to market rates of lending charges applied by financial institutions is to an important extent dependent on the functioning of credit markets. In a neo-classical financial environment without frictions and asymmetric information, that is, a world in which the Modigliani-Miller (1958) theorem holds, agents in the private sector can, at market interest rates, borrow and lend whatever amounts are necessary to achieve their desired spending patterns (Purvis, 1992). The absence of information imperfections between

---

[16] This issue could have important policy implications. If real rigidities do not vanish in the long run, and monetary policy consequently is non-neutral in the long run, this is a new element in the discussion regarding central bank independence. As this discussion is beyond the scope of this book, we will not take it up here.

suppliers and users of funds implies that the substitutability between internal and external financing sources and between different forms of external finance, such as intermediated and non-intermediated credit, is perfect (BIS, 1994). In this case, financial intermediaries play a purely passive role in the monetary transmission process, namely the channeling of short-term saving to longer-term investment projects. If bank assets and liabilities have identical characteristics to other borrowing and saving instruments, such as bonds, then bank and non-bank instruments will trade at the same price (assuming risk neutrality). The passthrough between market interest rates and bank rates is immediate and complete (Dale and Haldane,1993). Financial prices in this perfect capital market allocate financial quantities optimally. In this case, interactions between financial variables and non-financial activity can be reduced and simplified to interactions between interest rates and non-financial activity (Mauskopf, 1990; Mankiw and Romer, 1991).

An alternative view is that financial prices do not clear the credit market. This view of the transmission process is also known as the credit channel.[17] In this case the efficient functioning of the market for credit is hindered by asymmetries in information between borrowers and lenders, and in principal-agent problems (Oliner and Rudebusch, 1996). These problems lead to endogenous and varying credit conditions which help to shape the transmission of monetary policy decisions through the economy. As recognised by, *inter alia*, Kashyap, Stein and Wilcox (1993) and Dale and Haldane (1993), this uncertainty generates a potential important role for financial intermediaries which specialise in gathering and distilling agent-specific information. The implication is that financial intermediaries, usually banks, play an unique role in the monetary transmission process, acting as an interface between the policy decisions of the central bank and non-financial activity. Decisions of financial institutions regarding the size of their balance sheet and the yields paid on their assets and liabilities in this case play an active role in the transmission of monetary policies. Because financial institutions obtain a portion of their funds from instruments subject to reserve requirements, open market operations, which alter the quantity of reserves, may affect the opportunity cost of funds to those institutions beyond their impact on market interest rates. That is, financial quantities (the availability of credit) play an important role in the transmission mechanism. In this view of monetary transmission the impact of changes in market rates (price) on the cost of finance (which is price- as well as quantity-related) is dependent on (BIS, 1994, 1995):

- the behavioural characteristics of the economy, expressed in e.g. the

---

[17] For an extensive discussion of this channel see, for example, B. Friedman (1983); Bernanke (1983, 1993a,b); Kashyap and Stein (1994); Hubbard (1994b); Bernanke, Gertler and Gilchrist (1996); Friedman and Kuttner (1993); Bernanke and Gertler (1995).

balance sheet of private sector agents[18];
- the economy's financial structure such as, for example, the relative importance of financing at short-term versus long-term rates (which, among other things, depends on the prevalence of fixed versus variable rate financing);
- the relative importance of direct versus intermediated financing (Sijben, 1996).

The responses of longer-term interest rates to movements in short-term rates is easiest explained under the assumption of perfect capital markets made above. If all financial assets other than money[19] are perfect substitutes, there exists only one relative asset price, 'the' interest rate. The difference between the short-term interest rate and the long-term interest rate, or, more generally, changes in market interest rates along the maturity spectrum, will reflect fully the current level and expected future path of short-term interest rates (Mauskopf, 1990).[20] This is the so-called expectations theory of the term structure (Modigliani and Shiller, 1973). If substitution is not perfect[21], the differences between interest rates of different maturity will not only reflect expectations of future changes in short-term rates, but also risk premia (Perilleux and Wouters, 1994). We will return to this important channel of the transmission mechanism in the next chapter of this book.

Examining the second stage

The impact of changes in the cost of finance (which includes price- as well as quantity-related variables) on non-financial activity depends on various factors (Bank of England, 1990). First, changes in the cost of capital are

[18] This is sometimes denoted as the financial accelerator. It means that because of asymmetric information endogenous cyclical changes in the quality of the balance-sheet structure of borrowers (households and firms) can reinforce themselves, by influencing the development of net-worth and cash-flows of the borrower. See Bernanke, Gertler and Gilchrist (1996).

[19] We define money as the financial asset which is used primarily for transactions purposes, and has a rate of return that is exogenously fixed in nominal terms. For convenience, this nominal rate of return is set equal to zero. See Papademos and Modigliani (1990) for details.

[20] In other words, arbitrage ensures that, in each period of time, the expected return on the financial instrument that has n periods to maturity equals the return on rolling over (n-1 times) the financial instrument with 1 period remaining to maturity. See Tzavalis and Wickens (1996).

[21] Besides changing the relationship between short-term and long-term interest rates, allowing for imperfect substitutability between non-money financial assets requires a multi-asset 'portfolio balance' specification of asset equilibrium (Tobin, 1961, 1969; M. Friedman, 1959, 1970; Friedman and Schwartz, 1963; Brunner, 1971; Foley and Sidrauski, 1971; Sargent, 1979). This equilibrium determines not a single interest rate, but a vector of rates, representing the yields on bonds, equity and other assets. The transmission of changes in the instrument variables to the ultimate targets operating through this array of imperfect substitutes for money balances is sometimes denoted as the asset price channel (Mishkin, 1995, 1996).

relevant for the selection of new investment projects or portfolio investment, thereby affecting the opportunity cost of real expenditure decisions. This effect is called the substitution effect. Second, changes in the cost of finance lead to changes in average rates on outstanding contracts, modifying incomes and cash flows and hence constraints on spending. This effect is denoted as the income effect. Third, changes in the cost of finance affect the value of certain assets, such as housing, equities or government stocks. These values, in turn, have an impact on wealth perceptions, which influence spending. Moreover, this so-called wealth effect influences the ability to borrow and the willingness to lend. Referring to the discussion in the previous section, it can be seen that the magnitude of these factors *inter alia* depends on imperfections in the credit market. The exact impact of changes in the cost of finance on non-financial activity therefore depends on structural features such as balance sheet structure, in particular the relative and absolute size of liabilities at floating interest rates, either of the private or of the public sector (BIS, 1995).

A final factor through which changes in the cost of finance influences non-financial activity operates through the exchange rate (Menon, 1995). Under flexible exchange rates, a change in the domestic instrument variable *ceteris paribus* will elicit movements in the exchange rate. This will, in turn, have an impact on non-financial activity via, firstly, the passthrough to import and export prices and, secondly, the impact of changes in import and export prices on the current account. An alternative interpretation of the exchange rate channel is given in the sixth chapter of this study, where it is shown that pegging the exchange rate to a stable low-inflation foreign currency is a means to achieve price stability in the domestic country.[22] Price stability is achieved through a simple disciplining mechanism (Wellink, 1990; Svensson, 1994; Pech, 1994). First, if a higher domestic than foreign inflation occurs, it leads to a domestic real exchange rate appreciation, that is, domestic goods become more expensive relative to foreign goods. This reduces the demand for domestic goods and induces a cyclical downswing which will reduce the domestic inflation subsequently to the same long-run level as the foreign one (note that we have assumed imperfect price adjustment). Second, wage- and price-setting behaviour will to some extent anticipate these consequences of too high wage and price increases, which will make a higher domestic inflation less likely to occur in the first place.

Examining the third stage

Our discussion of the first and second stages of the monetary transmission

[22] In general, pegging the exchange rate is not a substitute for monetary stability and credibility at home. In fact, a peg is only sustainable when it is credible, and credibility is partly determined by domestic policies.

mechanism showed that, because of real rigidities in the form of credit market imperfections, monetary policy can influence non-financial activity not (only) through interest rates but (also) through the availability of credit. In addition, the extent to which changes in non-financial activity generated by changes in the instrument variables are translated into changes in prices and output, respectively, depends largely on the behaviour of wage and price setters. In general, the greater the degree of nominal wage and price flexibility, the more changes in non-financial activity affect prices and not output. Wage and price behaviour, in turn, is influenced by inflation expectations as well as by institutional factors. Following the introduction of the rational expectations hypothesis (Muth, 1961), to macroeconomics by Lucas (1972a,b), Sargent (1976) and Sargent and Wallace (1975), expectational effects are related to concepts like credibility and reputation of the policy maker.[23] The institutional framework in which this interaction between the policy maker and the private sector takes place stresses factors which inhibit the continuous clearing of markets. Rational expectations are thus compatible with non-market clearing due to various (institutional) barriers to rapid adjustment of prices and wages (Fischer, 1977; Blinder, 1991, 1994; Ball and Mankiw, 1994). New Keynesian economics provide explanations as regards the causes of these nominal rigidities (Ball, Mankiw and Romer, 1988; Mankiw and Romer, 1991).[24] In this respect a number of suggestions have been made (Barrell, 1990; Dréze and Bean, 1990; Layard, Nickell and Jackman, 1991; Egebo and Englander, 1992), which can be summarised as follows. The most notable structural factors contributing to the sluggishness of price adjustments are legal and institutional barriers to price adjustments (such as rent controls) and monopolistic or oligopolistic competition in product markets (Hall, 1986). But also in a competitive environment, price inertia may result from the existence of menu costs in changing prices or from a desire by firms not to damage long-term relationships with clients by frequent variations in prices (Blinder, 1991;1994). As regards wage rigidities, explanations also focus on factors hindering competition, such as regulatory impediments to wage adjustments (e.g. minimum wages), the influence of unions and generous unemployment benefit schemes.[25] On the other hand, even where competition is fierce but information is distributed asymmetrically, there may be a desire of both firms and workers to have longer-term working relationships entailing an implicit

[23] Seminal work in this field includes Kydland and Prescott (1977) and Barro and Gordon (1983).

[24] New Keynesian economics has evolved from providing microeconomic justifications for the models of the 1960's to models that explain how small barriers to full and immediate nominal adjustment and the real rigidities in the markets for labour, goods, and credit that cause those small barriers generate large movements in output and employment.

[25] For a recent discussion of rigidities in the labour market, see Akerlof, Dickens and Perry (1996).

insurance against excessive wage volatility, or firms may refrain from downward wage adjustments in order not to jeopardise employee motivation and labour productivity. Moreover, from the literature on hysteresis effects on unemployment (Cross, 1988), wage rigidities causing unemployment persistence are explained with insider-outsider and duration theories of the wage bargaining process (Blanchard and Summers, 1987).

Expectations and the transmission mechanism

From the literature initiated by Kydland and Prescott (1977) and Barro and Gordon (1983), it is clear that expectations of the public will ultimately determine the ability of the policy maker to achieve the ultimate target. From this it becomes clear that expectations play a crucial role in the monetary transmission mechanism. In turn these expectations are dependent on the public's assessment of the credibility of central bank behaviour. The latter concept is fundamental to modern analysis of monetary policy in general and central banking in particular (Fischer, 1994). Assessing alternative monetary policy strategies in terms of accountability and transparency, for example, as advocated by Shigehara (1996) and EMI (1997), can be motivated with the concept of credibility.

Expectations play an important role in each stage of the transmission mechanism. For example, expectations of economic agents largely determine the relationship between interest rates under the control of the policy maker and the rates most relevant for non-financial activity. Moreover, expectations of economic agents are important determinants of the future business cycle and are informative about future inflation. They furthermore play a key role in the international interdependence of important variables in various chains of the transmission mechanism. A detailed discussion of the role of expectations is presented in subsequent chapters. Here we want to stress the fact that the formation of expectations by itself is a manifestation of the existence of uncertainty.[26] We now turn to a discussion of the implications of the latter observation for monetary policy.

1.4 Implications for the foundations of monetary policy: a multi-model approach

From the preceeding discussions, it follows that a central conception for monetary policy is the transmission mechanism. As will be discussed further below, there exists considerable ambiguity regarding this mechanism. This ambiguity should, in our view, have consequences for the appropriate

[26] Another manifestation of the imperfect knowledge of the policy maker regarding the transmission mechanism is the use of indicator variables, as discussed in the second section.

methodology used by the monetary policy maker. The traditional approach of relying on a structural macroeconomic model to describe all aspects of the transmission mechanism and to answer every possible question, is less suitable. Instead, we suggest a more general framework for preparing monetary policy, in which a range of models is used to help analyse several pieces of information. The choice of model is determined by the specific problem to be analysed. This so-called multi-model approach allows the policy maker to grapple with the role of specific interactions in a comprehensible way. We believe that policy analysis using tools specifically designed to cope with the problem at hand increases the chances of finding stable relationships more than an analysis using a general (structural) model in which the specific circumstances can only be (imperfectly) translated into the general framework.

The ambiguity regarding monetary transmission is reflected in the well-known long and variable lags between actions by the policy maker in adjusting its instrument and the effects on inflation (M. Friedman, 1961; Blinder, 1997). Traditional determinants of these lags include a data collection lag, a recognition lag, a legislative lag, an implementation lag, and an impact lag. As a discussion of these determinants can be found in any textbook (see, for example, Hubbard, 1994a, pp. 684-685), we will not discuss them here.[27] Instead we wish to emphasize the role played by the theoretical uncertainty regarding the proper description of the transmission mechansim, the complexity of this mechanism, and the uncertainty with which economic agents participating in the transmission mechanism have to deal with. Since these factors are the main motivation for our proposed multi-model strategy, we will discuss them in more detail.

The analysis presented in the previous section indicates that there is no such thing as 'the unique' monetary transmission mechanism; there are various theoretical views. The resulting theoretical uncertainty is aggrevated by the complexity of the behavioural processes that together form the transmission mechanism. For instance, the rigidities mentioned in the previous section are important causes of the lags in monetary transmission, and the variability in these lags could result from differences in rigidities across countries and, due to institutional changes, in time, see Bryan and Gavin (1994). Moreover, differences between countries in structural factors, such as the foreign influence on the domestic economy, as well as the ongoing changes in these structural factors, play a role (Britton and Whitley, 1997).

In addition to the theoretical uncertainty regarding the transmission mechanism, and its complexity, the long and variable lags are caused by the

[27] In addition to these factors, Blinder (1997) argues that the fact that monetary policy decisions in many countries are made by a committee instead of a single person, also contributes to the lags in the effects of monetary policy.

changing perceptions of economic agents regarding the behaviour of the policy maker, the workings of the various stages of the process of monetary transmission and the 'correct' theory of the economic process. Such changes imply a certain amount of unpredictability in the behaviour of these agents. This uncertainty can be given two interpretations. The first relates to situations (of Knightian risk) in which the frequency approach to probability and uncertainty is valid. In this case, individual behaviour can be analysed with theories of expectations formation. Variable lags are consistent with most of these theories, including the rational expectations hypothesis. Under this hypothesis, variability of individual behaviour could result from heterogenous information sets and from new information becoming available at irregular intervals. Both factors could also account for variable lags in the second interpretation of uncertainty, in which the frequency approach as a general theory of uncertainty is rejected. This case, valid in situations of Knightian uncertainty and which we denote as fundamental uncertainty, is especially relevant for monetary economies as it provides a theoretical rationale for holding money, see Hoogduin (1991) and Van der Lecq (1996).[28] The existence of fundamental uncertainty acknowledges the limitations on the cognitive capacity of economic agents. These limitations imply that agents are not able to optimize over the entire range of possible actions, as implicit in the frequency approach (Lucas, 1977, p. 223). They introduce uncertainty in selecting most preferred alternatives, which will tend to produce errors and surprises. Such mistakes are by their nature unpredictable and erratic. Fundamental uncertainty can therefore not be removed; it is impossible to reduce all uncertainty to the probabilistic kind. People may acquire new information, deep structural parameters such as preferences, technology and risk aversion may change. These changes are an

[28] The distinction, due to Keynes (1936), between the formation of expectations and the incompleteness of the information on which these expectations are based, is of importance here (see also Hicks, 1974). The latter (a manifestation of fundamental uncertainty) determines the confidence economic agents attach to the former. The lower this confidence, the higher the uncertainty with which agents are confronted. In the face of uncertainty, economic agents may prefer not to commit themselves for too long a period (that is, make irreversible spending decisions), and delay their decisions until the moment they are sufficiently confident to rely on their knowledge (Hoogduin, 1991, p. 65). The existence of uncertainty thus creates a need for liquidity, and money is the most liquid of assets. Note the similarity in reasoning with the recent literature on investment behaviour which stresses the irreversible character of investment expenditure, in combination with the fact that these decisions can be delayed (Pindyck, 1991; Dixit and Pindyck, 1994; Dixit, 1995; Abel, Dixit, Eberly and Pindyck, 1996). According to this line of reasoning, the investment decision has option-like characteristics, and methods developed for pricing options in financial markets can be applied to the theory of investment behaviour. With respect to our study, the implication is that uncertainty regarding future sales and sales price prospects is an important determinant of the investment decision, and also contributes to the variability of lags in the transmission mechanism.

endogenous element of the transmission process, and can affect economic decisions at any moment (Hoogduin, 1991, p. 174). Relations between variables in the various stages of the transmission process and expectations may therefore change at any moment. This interpretation of inherent uncertainty in the transmission process could well explain why, despite a considerable amount of research regarding the lags in the effects on monetary policy (Tucker, 1966; Tanner, 1969, 1972, 1979; Howrey, 1969; Waud, 1975; Dieckheuer, 1974; Smith, 1972), we are lacking and probably will never succeed in developing a theory that consistently and coherently explains these lags: agents simply can not decipher all of the complexity of the decision problems they face.

It should perhaps be added that the existence of fundamental uncertainty is not at odds with the primary goal of our analysis, which is to provide the policy maker with *stable* relationships between key variables in different chains of the transmission mechanism. Fundamental uncertainty does not necessarily imply instability of behaviour. There exist counterforces which make for stability and make people confident that sensible decisions can be made (Hoogduin, 1991). Heiner (1983) argues that the more uncertain people are, the better predictable their behaviour is, because they employ the same rule in many different situations. Rules, conventions and laws, in combination with existing institutions, traditions and experience invoke a tendency towards stability in behaviour in the face of fundamental uncertainty. This is because allowing flexibility to react to information or to select actions will not necessarily improve performance if there is (fundamental) uncertainty about how to use that information or about when to select particular actions. Rules and conventions, among others, introduce some type of rigidity or inflexibility in adjusting to different situations, thereby limiting behaviour to a smaller set of repertoires that can be readily administered.

A number of clarifying remarks are in order. First, using several models is by no means an attempt to obscure policy makers' view of the transmission mechanism. It is merely the implication of the view that this mechanism is too complex to be captured in even a large model. Neither does this general framework imply rejecting the use of structural models in monetary policy; we merely propose supplementing the policy analysis with models of the reduced-form kind (Whitley, 1997). Second, the proposed underpinning of monetary policy has to be distinguished from the monetary policy strategy. Where the former pertains to the methods used to analyse information, the latter relates to the judgement by the policy maker of the information analysed, that is, the policy (re-)action. Both are related, of course, as the strategy followed in part determines the kind of questions to be analysed. But the policy maker will ultimately be judged by the success of his strategy in terms of achieving the ultimate target, and not on the analysis that underlies his judgement. Third, using a range of models implies the possibility of different outcomes, perhaps suggesting various policy reactions. How is the policy maker to choose? The answer lies in the policy strategy followed, which should provide him with a guidepost or benchmark for attributing weights to different outcomes. Whilst economic theory and quantitative information aid the policy maker by providing him with basic notions, the choice of strategy is part of knowledge that is very difficult to make explicit. This is because this choice reflects the reaction of the policy maker to fundamental uncertainty regarding the process of monetary transmission. As noted by Heiner (1983), such uncertainty requires behaviour of, in this case, the policy maker to be governed by mechanisms that restrict the flexibility to choose potential actions. These mechanisms, of which the monetary policy strategy is an example, simplify behaviour to less complex patterns, which are easier to observe and to predict. The choice of mechanism, that is of monetary strategy, is partly determined by institutions, traditions, experience, rules, conventions and laws. Monetary policy could, in this respect, at least in part be considered an art.

Models to be used in the multi-model approach

We argued above that the monetary policy maker is in need of a flexible methodology, in which all relevant information is analysed, not just the information relevant according to a particular theory that is incorporated in a structural model (Hall and Henry, 1988; Kashyap and Stein, 1994; Baumgartner et al., 1997).[29] The so-called reduced form models provide this flexibility. They study the behaviour of variables considered to be important in (channels of) the transmission mechanism under consideration, without imposing restrictions based on supposed *a priori* knowledge of the dynamic linkages between the variables. The models are reduced in the sense that they do not require explicit estimation of all the behavioural parameters of the participants in the transmission mechanism (Sims, 1982). Both the structural and reduced form approaches can best be viewed as complementary (Palm, 1988). This can be seen most easily for a prominent example of the reduced form approach, the so-called vector autoregression (VAR) analysis (Sims, 1980, 1982). As is well known (see Hamilton, 1994, for a formal exposition), the equations in a VAR-analysis can be viewed as the reduced form

[29] Other disadvantages of the structural modelling approach include the incredibility of the identifying restrictions used to obtain equation-by-equation interpretations of structural models (Sims, 1980). Moreover, it may not always be possible to construct these models, due to lack of data or prohibitive costs. Structural models are relatively expensive to construct and to maintain, and the estimation may entail computational inefficiencies (Van Loo, 1984; Knot, 1996). Another problem with large structural models is that they are so complex, and there are so many specific interactions, that the study of such models does not contribute much to our understanding of specific economic mechanisms.

equations of the variables in a structural model. The reduced form is therefore a condensed version of the underlying structural form.

Reduced forms are not without their problems, either. First, the main advantage of the reduced form over the structural model, that there are no *a priori* restrictions that limit the interdependencies of the variables included in the model (Garretsen and Swank, 1997), is, ironically, at the same time one of the major weaknesses of this approach: convincing identifying restrictions are hard to come by. Another drawback of reduced forms is the impossibility of making direct inferences on hypotheses derived from economic theory.[30] Although one can, in principle, deduce the structural form from the reduced form given the proper identifying restrictions (Cramer, 1988), in practice these restrictions are unavailable. In that case there is no one-to-one correspondence between the reduced and the structural form, and a particular reduced form may be compatible with different structural models (representing different economic theories). These limitations of reduced forms illustrate the need to complement them with structural models (Kuipers, 1983, Buiter, 1988 and Woodford, 1994).[31]

The aim of this study is to provide the policy maker with stable, economically interpretable, relationships which can be used for monetary policy purposes. In trying to achieve this goal, we have to deal with the fact that the current theoretical knowledge of the monetary transmission mechanism and the lags in this mechanism is imperfect and the data which have to be used to put this limited knowledge to the test empirically, are deficient. Given these problems, it seems advisable not to burden our analysis with unduly rigid priors. The reduced form methodology allows us to pick up unexpected patterns and correlations, without being constrained by a theory that may or may not be plausible. For a recent discussion of the reduced form methodology in a monetary policy context, see Leeper, Sims and Zha (1996). The reduced form approach thus provides us with shortcuts, where complementary structural models present a broad overview. The former can be especially useful compared with the latter when specific questions are to be addressed, or when new information has to be evaluated in a relatively short time span. The speedy processing of new information is especially important given the uncertainties surrounding the linkages in the transmission mechanism. These uncertainties make it necessary for the policymaker to continuously assess the effect of the change in instrument in different stages of the process of monetary transmission, and, when necessary (and possible), make adjustments.

---

[30] However, see Basmann (1972) and Kloek (1988) for a critical assessment of the role played by theory in macroeconomic structural models.

[31] Examples of the use of the structural modelling approach in the context of the transmission mechanism include Mauskopf (1990), Bryant, Hooper and Mann (1983), Smets (1995) and Ball (1997).

1.5 Topics studied

The suggested general framework for preparing monetary policy consists of a number of different models. In the chapters that follow we will illustrate this approach with a number of case studies, pertaining to different stages in the transmission mechanism.[32] The subjects of these studies can be grouped in two categories, which are important from a theoretical perspective, i.e. international interdependencies and expectations.

The emphasis on international linkages contrasts with the contributions of Poole (1970) or Papademos and Modigliani (1990), which focus on closed economies. Henderson and McKibbin (1993) develop a multiregion model which allows for interregional linkages. Roper and Turnovsky (1980) modify the analysis of Poole to a single open economy.[33] However, using only structural models these authors are forced to make restrictive assumptions, in order to keep the discussion tractable. In this study, we investigate the foreign influence on three specific elements of the transmission mechanism. These are:

- the domestic long-term interest rate (chapter three),
- the domestic business cycle (chapter four)
- the domestic inflation rate (chapter six).

The purpose is to examine how foreign variables to a great extent influence domestic variables which are considered to be key variables in various channels of the transmission process, sometimes reducing the scope of domestic monetary policy authorities to influence their (domestic) target variables.

In our discussion of the role of expectations, we make extensive use of survey data, in which private sector economic agents are asked to express their expectations concerning future prices, output and exchange rates. These data allow us to derive explicit expressions for important expectational variables. The effects of expectations are discussed with respect to three important variables, each pertaining to different stages of the transmission mechanism. More specifically, we discuss:

- the information content of expectations concerning future inflation and output reflected in the term structure of interest rates for monetary policy decisions (chapter two);
- the role of exchange rate expectations in the relationship between domestic and foreign interest rates (chapter three);
- the usefulness of explicit measures of inflation expectations of

---

[32] We acknowledge that we do not provide a complete discussion of all the chains in the transmission mechanism. Our analysis is therefore partial by definition.

[33] Recent work along similar lines include Aizenman and Frenkel (1986); Frankel and Chinn (1991) and Asako and Wagner (1992).

consumers for the direct inflation targeting strategy for monetary policy (Svensson, 1996; Green, 1996) (chapter five).

2. THE INFORMATION CONTENT OF THE YIELD CURVE FOR MONETARY POLICY: A SURVEY[1]

2.1 Introduction

Price stability is now generally accepted as the main policy goal of monetary policy. Because the relationship between the main instrument variable used, the short-term interest rate, and the final policy goal is blurred by long and variable lags, less consensus exists regarding the question of how to use the instrument to achieve this final objective (i.e. the strategy). Friedman's (1993, 1994) distinction between intermediate targets and information variables is useful in this respect. The intermediate targeting procedure calls for automatic changes in the instruments in reaction to unexpected movements of the variable selected as the intermediate target. The key role of the intermediate target variable is thus to provide the central bank with a ready rule for processing and acting on new information (Friedman and Kuttner, 1996). As described by Poole (1970), and elaborated by, e.g., Papademos and Modigliani (1990), the optimal choice of the intermediate target depends on the nature of disturbances influencing the economy. Possible candidates are interest rates (the stabilization of which was the central tenet of monetary policy in the Keynesian era), money supply growth (the targeting of which is central in the monetarist line of thought), the exchange rate and the expected inflation rate (in the recently developed direct inflation targeting strategy).[2]

In the face of financial deregulation and innovation as well as integration and globalisation of financial markets the relationship between the financial sector and the real economy became more complicated (Friedman, 1993). These major changes in the preconditions for monetary policy undermined the use of intermediate targets for monetary policy (Crockett, 1993, 1994). It is no longer generally true that unexpected movements in the variable selected as the intermediate target necessarily convey information about the policy goal that warrants a policy change. In other words, the automatic pilot interpretation of the intermediate targeting procedure is no longer valid. The latter argument is central in the second approach, the information variable procedure. By this we mean a judgmental or discretionary procedure in which unexpected movements of selected information variables are analysed to determine whether they warrant action

---

[1] Reprinted from *De Economist*, 146 (2), (1998), J.M. Berk, "The Information Content of the Yield Curve for Monetary Policy: a survey", 303 – 320 © 1998 with kind permission from Kluwer Academic Publishers.

[2] Svensson (1996) shows that, in contrast to what is suggested by its name, 'direct' inflation targeting implies inflation forecast targeting: the central bank's inflation forecast becomes the intermediate target.

by the central bank. This procedure usually reflects a systematic response by policy makers; it is therefore not taken to imply randomness in decision-making. It is because there is no rule which prescribes the central bank how to react to deviations of a particular information variable from its expected path that the procedure is labelled discretionary. Although different in concept, the dividing lines between both strategies are not so clear in the day-to-day implementation of monetary policy. The temporal aspect of the reviewing of intermediary targets is of crucial importance here. The shorter the review period (that is the length of time for which the intermediate target is in force), the more the intermediate targeting and the information variable procedures tend to coincide.

Another implication of the abovementioned changes in the (inter)national financial markets[3] was that in some countries the variable which was previously selected as the intermediate target, the quantity of money, no longer functioned as a reliable predictor for all aspects of overall economic activity that are of interest for purposes of monetary policy.[4] There is thus a need for additional information variables which are predictably linked to non-financial activity. We define the latter to include inflation (logically linked to the ultimate objective of monetary policy, price stability) and real economic activity. The latter is also of interest for a central bank since monetary actions undertaken to safeguard the objective of price stability in the face of disturbances can elicit real economic effects in the short run, especially when the degree of credibility of monetary policy is low (Sijben, 1994; Fuhrer, 1997). In this chapter we concentrate on one possible information variable, the term structure of interest rates. Our objective is to review the information content of the term structure of interest rates[5] with respect to future movements in inflation and real output, and to investigate whether this yield curve is useful for monetary policy purposes. In the past two decades, a good deal of theoretical and empirical work has been done

[3] This is not to say that these changes are the sole reason for the loss of predictive power of money. See Friedman and Kuttner (1996) for an extensive discussion.

[4] Financial innovation led to the introduction of near monies and advanced the process of financial disintermediation (Sijben, 1995). In combination with liberalisation of international capital markets and deregulation of financial markets this created a range of new substitutes for financial assets included in the targeted monetary aggregates (Shigehara, 1996). The result was a trade-off between stability of money demand and controllability of the monetary aggregate by the central bank: the demand for broadly defined money (which is less controllable by the central bank) is more stable than the demand for narrow money. See Fase and Winder (1993) for details.

[5] We define the term structure as the relation between the yields to maturity for different terms to maturity. Here we use the terms 'term structure' and 'yield curve' in an interchangeable fashion, which is, strictly speaking, not correct: the term structure is a particular yield curve (i.e. for zero-coupon bonds). See Shiller (1990), Svensson (1994) and Haubrich and Dombrosky (1996) for a discussion, and Deacon and Derry (1994) and Shich (1996) for details concerning the construction and estimation of various yield curves.

regarding the information contained in the term structure. Although the empirical research has been mainly directed at G-7 countries, recent work by, *inter alia*, Bernard and Gerlach (1996), Gerlach and Smets (1995), Koedijk and Kool (1995), and the fourth chapter of this study presents evidence for the Netherlands. Given this preponderance of (recent) research, we do not present additional empirical evidence here. The contribution of this chapter instead is to make a comprehensive and critical survey of the main results that have been accomplished by research on the information content of the term structure. In particular, we combine the results of existing work on the relationship between the term structure and, respectively, the future inflation rate and real economic activity. This is convenient, as both lines of inquiry have been discussed separately in the literature. Moreover, the combination seems also preferable from a theoretical point of view, as inflation and growth are, of course, not independent. As we will show, the empirical results can be in part explained by this interdependency.

The remainder of the chapter is organised as follows. In the second section, we discuss theories of the yield curve to determine why this concept should possess any information content. The third section investigates whether these theories have empirical validity. The fourth section concentrates on three basic considerations which determine the usefulness of the yield curve for monetary policy: stability, predictability and controllability. The fifth section concludes.

2.2 Theories of the yield curve

In this section, we present theoretical arguments as to why the yield curve possesses information content. A critical discussion of these theories is deferred to the fourth section, after a review of their empirical validity.[6]

2.2.1 Yield curve and future inflation rates

We define the information content with regard to future inflation as the ability of the slope of the yield curve (the yield spread) to predict the change in the future inflation rate. We concur with Mishkin (1990a, 1990b), who remarks that this is a narrow interpretation of the information content since no use is made of additional economic variables in combination with the slope of the yield curve. This criticism notwithstanding, we follow existing practice by using this interpretation.

---

[6] In addition to the yield spread as defined above, there exist other interest rate spreads which also have information content. Friedman and Kuttner (1992, 1993), for example, discuss the information content of the differential between the rate on commercial paper and the rate on Treasury Bills with regard to future inflation as well as future economic activity.

The theoretical basis for the abovementioned information content consists of the combination of the Fisher equation and the preferred habitat theory of the yield curve (Modigliani and Sutch, 1966). The (one-period) Fisher equation decomposes the one-period nominal interest rate roughly into an one-period *ex ante* real interest rate and thé inflation expected one period ahead.[7] The preferred habitat theory of the yield curve is based on the arbitrage condition that, after adjusting for risk, the expected return from holding for one period a bond that has *n*-periods to maturity is the same as the certain return from a one-period bond. Combining these theories gives us the following expression (for a formal derivation, see Tzavalis and Wickens, 1996):

$$R(n,t) = E_t r(n,t) + E_t \pi(n,t) + \phi(n,t) \tag{1}$$

where $R(n,t)$ denotes the yield to maturity at t of a bond with *n*-periods to maturity. E is the expectations operator, and the subscript pertains to the period in which the expectation is formed, using information up to and including t. $r(n,t)$ is the average real interest rate over the current and next n-1 periods, $\pi(n,t)$ is the average inflation rate over the next n periods and $\phi(n,t)$ is the average risk premium on an *n*-period bond until it matures. All rates are expressed in natural logarithms, save for the inflation rate, which is defined as the first difference of two logarithms.

Equation (1) can be interpreted as an *n*-period Fisher equation. Subtracting from (1) the (similar) *m*-period Fisher equation gives the slope of the yield curve between segments n and m. For m=1 (the spot rate), the following equation emerges:

$$R(n,t) - R(1,t) = E_t\left[r(n,t) - r(1,t)\right] + E_t\left[\pi(n,t) - \pi(1,t)\right] + \phi(n,t) - \phi(1,t) \tag{2}$$

It follows from (2) that the slope of the yield curve (left hand side) will provide information on the expected real interest rate spread (sometimes denoted as the term structure of real interest rates), the market's expected inflation path (i.e. the change in the future *n*-period inflation rate from the 1-period inflation rate) and variation in risk premia. There thus exists a potential identification problem: if these variables are not all perfectly correlated, the yield spread is a noisy forecast of any of them. Mishkin (1990b, pp. 79-80) states that the slope of the yield curve will provide an

[7] In a more general form the Fisher equation also incorporates an inflation risk premium and the conditional variance of inflation. These factors - which are quantitatively unimportant (Tzavalis and Wickens, 1996, p.105) - are omitted here for expositional ease.

exact measure of the market's expected inflation path if and only if all the following restrictive assumptions are satisfied: (i) the expected real interest rate is constant over time (horizontal real term structure), (ii) expectations are formed rationally and (iii) risk premia are constant over time. The first assumption causes the first term on the right hand side of (2) to vanish. The second assumption implies the unpredictability of forecast errors of inflation at the moment that the expectation is formed (that is, errors in the inflation rates expected at *t* to occur during the life of the bond, are uncorrelated; see Mishkin, 1991). The third assumption justifies neglecting the last term on the right hand side. Violation of any of these assumptions makes the interpretation of the yield curve more complex and reduces its value in forecasting changes in future inflation. Following current practice (see, for example, Campbell, 1982, Campbell and Shiller, 1987, Hardouvelis, 1988, Jondeau and Ricart, 1996) we combine assumptions (ii) and (iii) above, and refer to this combination as the expectations theory of the term structure.[8]

Equation (2) can be interpreted as a (semi) reduced form of a dynamic macro-economic model where both short-term and long-term interest rates are jointly determined. The foundation of this interpretation lies in finance theory, following the work of, inter alia, Merton (1973), Vasicek (1977), Lucas (1978), Dothan (1978), Breeden (1979), Cox, Ingersoll and Ross (1981, 1985a, 1985b) and Hu (1993), who studied the term structure of interest rates within a stochastic general equilibrium model.[9] Shiller (1990) concludes that, whilst offering various insights in theoretical finance, these models are difficult to implement empirically.[10] Turnovsky (1985, 1989) extends the abovementioned models to address policy issues. He embeds the expectations theory of the yield curve in a new classical rational expectations general equilibrium macroeconomic model, based on maximizing behaviour on the part of homogeneous agents operating in frictionless markets, and analyzes the effects of various monetary and fiscal policies on the term structure. Such a model provides us with a relationship between the nominal yield spread and future changes in inflation similar to equation (2) under assumptions (i)-(iii) above.

2.2.2 Yield curve and future economic activity

In the new classical models mentioned above, there is no predictive value of the yield spread with respect to future economic activity: prices adjust

---

[8] For a discussion of the expectations theory, see Cox, Ingersoll and Ross (1981).

[9] Most popular among these are the so-called uni-factor models, in which the prices of bonds of all maturities depend on a single random explanatory factor, e.g. the spot interest rate. For an example of a multi-factor model, see Brennan and Schwartz (1979).

[10] For example, the theoretical models are formulated in continuous time. See Chan, Karolyi, Longstaff and Sanders (1992) for an empircal assessment of these models.

instantaneously. On the other extreme, if prices are fixed, then nominal yield spreads are a reflection of real spreads, which contain information regarding future real economic activity (Mishkin, 1990a, 1991).[11] When price adjustments are not instantaneous, the theoretical relationship between the yield spread and real economic activity is not clear-cut. As can be seen from a standard IS-LM model for a small open economy (see, for example, Dornbusch, 1980, pp. 175-192; Blanchard and Fischer, 1989, pp. 532-536), the nature of the relationship between yield slope and future real activity depends on the nature of the shocks hitting the economy and the speed of price adjustment.[12] In the presence of real economic shocks and sticky prices, a positive yield spread is indicative of a future economic upswing. On the other hand, when monetary shocks dominate, a positive yield spread indicates a weakening of future economic activity. In the former case the expected outward shift of the IS-curve raises expected future short term rates (because the expected increase in income raises money demand), and this expectation is translated into higher current long-term rates. The information content is thus based on the expected effects of a real-economic disturbance on interest rates. In the latter case, a monetary shock such as the expectation of a future monetary tightening also raises future short-term rates and current long-term rates, but the resulting steepening of the yield curve now indicates a future decline in economic activity. The information content reflects the expected effects of monetary policy via interest rates on economic activity. When prices are flexible in the short run, the abovementioned analysis of shocks becomes more complicated because we have to take inflation expectations into account. In reaction to the monetary shock future real short-term rates will increase, but, if monetary policy is considered to be credible, future nominal short-term rates can decline, especially for those expected to prevail in the more distant future. With a credible monetary policy, the yield spread will decline and will be indicative of a future increase in economic activity: the relationship will again be positive.[13]

---

[11] Mishkin interprets the real yield spread (long minus short) as the difference between long-run and short-run marginal productivity of capital. When the peak of the business cycle is reached, productive potential is fully used, short run capital productivity is high *vis-à-vis* capital productivity in the longer run, when activity is expected to weaken. When the trough is reached, current capital productivity is low, but the expectation of a future upswing implies higher long-run productivity. Thus the real yield spread and the future business cycle are positively related (Stokman,1991). An alternative theoretical explanation of a (positive) relationship between the real yield spread and future real activity is presented by Harvey (1988) with the use of the CAPM. See, however, Fase (1997) for a critical discussion of the CAPM.

[12] In this model, spending decisions are influenced by the long term rate, money market equilibrium by the short-term rate, and the long term rate by expected future short-term rates.

[13] The analysis of fiscal shocks also becomes more complicated when price adjustments

But, of course, inflation and real activity are not independent. The extreme positions of perfect price flexibility and complete price rigidity reflect a debate about adjustment processes (about whether quantities or prices adjust to a change in macroeconomic conditions) and with what speeds. A synthesis is offered in the New Keynesian approach (Blanchard and Fischer, 1989, pp. 372-504). Using models of imperfect competition, strategic behaviour in the face of information asymmetries and search and contracting models, sluggish price adjustments in labour and product markets are explained as outcomes of rational behaviour (Hall, 1986; Lindbeck and Snower, 1987; Layard et al., 1991; Cross, 1988; Christiano, Eichenbaum and Evans, 1996). The approach is a synthesis as it explains phenomena that are at odds with new-classical notions (such as rigidities) from principles such as individual optimising behaviour, as new-classicals do. It thereby provides a theoretical description which subsumes both abovementioned positions as extreme cases (Frank, 1986). Both can occur simultaneously, depending on particular institutional and structural characteristics of the economy. The implication is that the yield curve in general possesses information content regarding both future inflation and future economic activity, but that this content could differ across countries and in time.

2.3 The empirical validity of different theories[14]

This section reviews the literature regarding empirical tests of the different theories outlined above. We make the distinction between the yield curve as a predictor of future inflation changes and as a predictor of future economic activity, because both lines of inquiry have been studied separately in the literature. We moreover distinguish between maturity spreads of different lengths, as the empirical studies indicate that the outcomes are sensitive to variations in this length.

2.3.1 The information content with respect to future inflation

In section 2.1 it was concluded that the information content of the yield curve with respect to future changes in inflation can be represented as a composite

have to be taken into account. See Blanchard and Fischer (1989, p. 536) for a discussion.

[14] This review chapter ignores the - rather complex - econometric issues involved in an empirical investigation of the information content of the yield curve (see Hansen and Hodrick, 1980, for a discussion). Therefore we neglect an important proviso that frequently emerges in the literature on the information content, namely that the results are in general very sensitive to the econometric methodology chosen to calculate the yield curve and to extract information from this curve.

hypothesis of the expectations theory of the yield curve and constancy of the real interest rate. In reviewing the empirical research on this composite hypothesis we distinguish between studies for the US, which is the subject of most of the research, and for European countries.

US data

The seminal paper in the empirical analysis of the information content of the yield curve is Campbell and Shiller (1987). Using data from the far end of the yield curve they show that the composite hypothesis is easily rejected for the sample period 1959-1983. The same authors (Campbell and Shiller, 1991), using a longer sample period (1952-1987), generalised this result to almost any pair of maturities. However, rejection of the null hypothesis does not imply that the alternative (no information content) is true as the rejection could, among other factors, be specific for the estimation method chosen. This is in line with Fama (1990), who, based on an analysis of data for the period 1953-1989, concludes that the yield curve contains information about real interest rates, expected inflation rates and term premia, but that problems occur in isolating the information in the term structure about any one of them. Subsequent authors concentrate on the latter problem. Mishkin (1990a, 1990b) and Hardouvelis (1988), using datasets similar to the one used by Fama (1990), find that there is much more information in the term structure about future inflation at longer maturities than there is at shorter maturities. They attribute this to the inappropriateness of the assumption of constancy of the slope of the term structure of real interest rates.[15] This variability is the greatest at the short end and obscures the predictive power of the shorter maturity yield spread. In contrast, for the longer maturities the variation of the slope of the real term structure is much less, so that the yield spread at these maturities has a significant information content. Fama and Bliss (1987), using data for the period 1964-1985, indeed find some empirical evidence for this, but, as Hardouvelis (1994) notes, it is hard to think of a simple and plausible economic story that could explain this behaviour of real interest rates. Recent research (Tzavalis and Wickens, 1996), using a more recent data set (1978-1991), is even more negative regarding the information content with respect to future inflation. They conclude that the forecasting ability of the term spread is very poor. Moreover, they find no support for the previous finding that the information content increases with the length of the

---

[15] It can be shown analytically, see for instance Mishkin (1990b) and Jorion and Mishkin (1991), that the information content of the yield curve is a non-linear function of (i) how variable the expected inflation change is relative to the variability of the slope of the real term structure and (ii) the correlation of the expected inflation change with the variability of the slope of the real term structure. A large variability of changes in real interest rates relative to the variability of expected inflation changes and a negative correlation between changes in the real interest rates and the expected inflation diminishes the information content with respect to future inflation changes.

maturity spread.

Data on other countries[16]

To investigate whether the abovementioned results are country-specific, we review the empirical outcomes for other countries. On average, the results are mixed. Some studies show that the US is no exception, finding that the information content depends on the empirical validity of the assumption of constancy of real interest rates. So Mishkin (1991) and Jondeau and Ricart (1996), using data on the shorter maturity term structure in ten OECD countries and France and Germany, respectively, conclude that the slope of the yield curve does not possess any information content. In contrast, Jorion and Mishkin (1991), Robertson (1992), Gerlach (1995) and Schich (1996) find that the term structure at long maturities has significant ability to forecast changes in inflation in the UK, Switzerland and Germany. Gerlach (1996) employs data on short-term and long-term interest rates for the G-10 countries, Australia, Austria and Spain to assess the information content of the yield curve, using the methodology developed by Campbell and Shiller (1987, 1991). He finds that the composite hypothesis is accepted for Australia, Canada, France, Germany, Japan, Switzerland, the UK and the Netherlands. For the other countries the hypothesis of information content is rejected.

Others, however, find that the US is an exceptional case. Gerlach and Smets (1995), using data on the short end of the maturity spectrum for 17 countries, find that the yield curve does possess information content. In fact, the only country for which the composite hypothesis is rejected, is the US. They attribute this to a lack of predictability of the short-term rate, but fail to give an economic explanation of this phenomenon. As predictability can be the manifestation of a credible monetary policy, differences in the information content across countries and in time could be a reflection of differences in the credibility of monetary policy. We will return to this in a next section. The relatively isolated position of the US is corroborated by Hardouvelis (1994), who studied the behaviour of 3-month and 10-year rates in the G-7 countries. He found evidence that the (10 year minus 3 months) spread has a significant information content for all countries except the US. For that country the yield spread correctly incorporates the information about expectations of future interest rates, but the market's expectations themselves violate the definition of rational expectations. This causes the rejection of the composite hypothesis for the US, even in the longer maturity spectrum studied. Koedijk and Kool (1995) study the information content of different yield spreads across seven countries and for different sample periods. In

[16] As different authors study different countries which differ in data availability, sample periods analysed differ widely in the studies reviewed. For this reason, we do not report the sample periods here.

contrast to Jorion and Mishkin (1991), which is their benchmark, they reject the composite hypothesis for all countries, mainly because of a violation of the assumption of constant real interest rates.

In sum, our review of the literature on the information content of the yield curve leads us to conclude that the empirical relationship between the yield curve and expected future inflation is complicated, and specific for a particular segment of the yield curve studied, as well as for the specific periods and countries analysed. The simple new classical theoretical explanation of the relationship between the yield spread and expected future changes in inflation is refuted by the data, mainly because of non-constancy of the slope of the real term structure. Prices adjust gradually and not instantaneously, thereby giving room for information content of the yield slope with respect to future real activity.

2.3.2 The information content with respect to future real activity

Estrella and Hardouvelis (1991) is one of the first detailed studies in this respect. They find that, for the US, the slope of the yield curve is positively related to future economic activity, and that it has extra predictive power over other leading indicators. The (*ex post*) forecasting power of the yield curve was especially strong in the 1970's and early 1980's, but rather weak in the most recent period. These results are, by and large, confirmed by and extended to other countries by others. Harvey (1991) and Ragnitz (1994) present evidence that the slope of the yield curve has a significant ability to predict future GNP growth in Germany, and Davis and Henry (1994) confirm this conclusion and extend it to the UK. Hu (1993) finds a significant positive relationship between the yield curve slope and future economic growth in the G-7 countries. This is confirmed by Estrella and Mishkin (1996) for the US. Moersch (1996), using data for the G-7 countries excluding France and Italy, also finds that the yield curve predicts future output successfully. Moreover, he corroborates the earlier finding of Hardouvelis (1991) that the yield spread in the US retains its predictive power for output after controlling for the short-term interest rate (which is used as a proxy for current monetary policy). The implication is that the yield spread also contains information about other variables than current monetary policy. Sauer and Scheide (1995), analysing data for France, Germany and Italy, examine the information content of the yield curve after controlling for the money stock. They find information content only for Germany. Clinton (1994) finds that the slope of the yield curve has good predictive power for future growth in Canadian output. In the fourth chapter of this study, we construct composite leading indicators for 16 industrialised countries and in most of them (i.e. for 10 out of the 16 countries studied) statistical tests suggest that the yield spread should be included. Moreover, in nearly all cases the yield curve retained its leading indicator properties when short-term rates were also included, thereby generalizing the results of Hardouvelis (1991) and Moersch (1996). Davis and Fagan (1994), analysing the EU countries, confirm the information content of the yield curve regarding future growth and report that it is quite robust across countries. Estrella and Mishkin (1995) study the ability of the yield curve to predict recessions in France, Germany, Italy, the UK and the US. They find that the term structure predicts recessions quite well in the US and Germany, and to a lesser degree in the UK and Italy. Bernard and Gerlach (1996) extend the work of Estrella and Mishkin (1995) to Belgium, Canada, Japan and the Netherlands. Although the information content is the highest in Canada, Germany and the US, the slope of the yield curve provides information about the likelihood of a future recession in all eight countries studied. The international differences in information content are explained by these authors in terms of differences in the regulation of financial markets. In a recent paper, Haubrich and Dombrosky (1996) conclude for the US that the yield spread has had substantial predictive power over the past 30 years, but that it has been less successful over the past decade, thereby confirming earlier findings of Estrella and Hardouvelis (1991). They contend that this deterioration is due to a structural change in the relationship between the yield curve and real economic activity.

In sum, based on a review of the existing empirical literature one can conclude that there exists a consensus that the slope of the yield curve possesses a considerable information content with respect to future economic activity. A steep curve is indicative of a future economic upswing. The explanations for this information content could be twofold, as discussed in section 2, and depend on the degree of price flexibility and the nature of shocks hitting the economy. Positive correlation between the yield spread and future real activity is consistent with either the expected effects of non-monetary shocks on interest rates or, under short-term price flexibility, to the expected effects of credible monetary policy, via interest rates, on real activity.

2.4 Implications for monetary policy

How could the central bank use the information content of the yield curve? Following Shigehara (1996) and Groeneveld et al. (1996), we address this question in the context of three basic conditions: stability, predictability and controllability. The first condition implies that the relationship between the yield curve and non-financial activity needs to be stable. The second condition states that the yield curve should possess leading indicator properties with respect to non-financial activity: observable developments of the yield curve must provide accurate 'advance knowledge' of non-financial activity. Controllability implies that the central bank must be able to control the yield curve precisely and fairly quickly. The latter condition is necessary only if the central bank wants to use the yield curve as intermediate target for monetary policy. Taken together, these conditions determine whether the central bank can use the information contained in the yield spread in an effective way.

Because the central bank can only determine the short-term interest rate to a large extent, the yield curve is not controllable by the central bank, which precludes using the former as an intermediate target (Bernanke and Blinder, 1992). We therefore focus on the stability of the relationship between the yield spread and future non-financial activity, in order to establish whether the yield curve can function as an information variable as defined by Friedman (1993, 1994). Although these are largely empirical issues, theoretical arguments are also of importance.

The previous sections illustrated that the empirical evidence on the information content of the yield curve is mixed and less clear-cut than the new classical theoretical explanation would lead us to believe: the composite hypothesis of constant real interest rates and the expectations theory of the yield curve is refuted by the data. The relationship between the yield curve and future changes in inflation was shown to be highly dependent on the countries studied, the sample period studied and the segment of the yield curve chosen. This implies that, although there is significant information in the yield curve about the future path of inflation in some countries, for some periods and for some segments of the yield curve, the relationship between yield spread and future inflation changes is not stable. On the other hand, a stable relationship seems to exist between the yield spread and future economic activity. The yield curve thus contains information regarding future price as well as real output movements, a proposition which might be consistent with New Keynesian principles. Taken together, the central bank should be cautious in using the yield curve as an information variable for policy purposes. Although the empirical evidence in general seems to indicate a positive correlation between the yield slope and non-financial activity, this correlation may be a reflection of different economic phenomena, each warranting different policy reactions. First, a steepening can indicate an upward revision of inflationary expectations, in which case a monetary tightening is called for. Second, the steepening may reflect the expectation of an increase in capital productivity, higher real interest rates and an increase in activity. In this case, a tightening may or may not be warranted, depending on the current state of the business cycle. Third, a positive correlation may reflect the expectation of a future monetary tightening by a credible monetary policymaker. The possibility of multiple valid theoretical explanations of a single observed relationship corroborates the findings of Turnovsky (1985; 1989) and McCallum (1994), who conclude that the response of the term structure is highly sensitive to the nature of the underlying shocks impinging on the economy.

There are also other reasons why central banks should be cautious in using the yield curve for monetary policy purposes. As Mishkin (1991) notes, the information content is sensitive to the relative variability of expected future inflation changes and changes in real interest rates, as well as to the correlation between changes in these two variables. Any change in the conduct of monetary policy, such as using the yield curve as an information variable, i.e. a guide for monetary policy, is likely to change the correlation and relative variability of changes in expected future inflation and in real interest rates. The forecasting quality of the yield curve for the path of future inflation could therefore change dramatically, making the yield slope a poor guide for monetary policy. This is, of course, an example of the Lucas (1976) critique. Similar arguments can be used to explain the observed differences in the information content across countries and in time. According to Gerlach and Smets (1995), the information content is largest in countries where short-term interest rates are easiest to predict. As noted earlier, predictability can be a manifestation of a credible monetary policy. Regime shifts can destroy this credibility (especially if they occur frequently), causing the behaviour of economic agents to change, which has consequences for the empirical validity of the information content. In a similar fashion, central banks in different countries can pursue identical policies, but, because of differences in credibility, this policy can induce different behaviour of economic agents across countries. The implication is that the information content of the yield curve differs across countries

A final problem with the use of the yield spread as information variable can be deduced from equation (2). From this equation it follows that the slope of the yield curve, while perhaps suggestive of the direction of market inflation expectations, by itself says little about the level of such expectations or of actual inflation now or in the future. A particular yield spread could therefore be consistent with multiple levels of future inflation rates.

Two caveats have to be made. First, some of the abovementioned objections regarding the information content of the yield curve, such as the implications of the Lucas (1976) critique, are also applicable to other variables, such as monetary aggregates. Second, our results are contingent on the rather narrow definition of information content used in this study (see section 2.1). It could be the case that the information content of the yield spread would improve considerably when use is made of other variables in combination with the slope of the yield curve.

2.5 Concluding remarks

This chapter discussed the information content of the yield curve regarding future inflation as well as future economic activity. Analysing the information content in general is of interest because deregulation, globalisation and innovation in international financial markets made it increasingly difficult for a central bank to continue previously successful policy strategies like intermediate targeting in the strict sense, that is, using the target as an automatic pilot. In addition, there was a need for additional information concerning future price and business cycle movements over and above that contained in traditional variables as monetary aggregates.

We presented theoretical arguments to explain the relationship between the yield curve and changes in future inflation and economic growth. We then reviewed the empirical validity of these arguments. It turned out that the empirical evidence in support of the yield spread having predictive power regarding future inflation changes is not stable. The opposite was the case for the yield curve as predictor of future economic activity. However, the theoretical interpretation of the latter relationship was shown to be ambiguous. The reason is that the response of the yield curve is sensitive to the nature of the underlying shocks hitting the economy and by institutional and structural factors influencing the speed of price adjustments. Different economic phenomena could lie behind the same observed movement in the yield spread, and the proper monetary policy response could, in principle, be different for these phenomena. This leads to the conclusion that caution must be exercised in using the yield curve as an information variable for monetary policy. A possible suggestion, and an interesting topic for future research, would be to investigate the possibilities for using the term structure to corroborate findings from other sources, e.g., forecasts from structural macroeconomic models, which are based on a broader information set.

Our review also showed that some of the objections raised against the yield spread are not specific for this variable. Therefore, as a corrolary, we wish to point out the importance of the Lucas (1976) critique in evaluating the information content of any variable. Even if there are convincing theoretical arguments, which are then validated by empirical results, the previously existing empirical relationship between the information variable and objectives of monetary policy could be destroyed when the central bank changes its conduct of monetary policy and the rational public will adjust its expectations (and changes its behaviour) accordingly. A possible solution would be for the central bank to take a wide range of information variables into account, thereby varying the importance given to the individual variables, depending on the particular circumstances. In this view, advocated by Friedman (1993, 1994), the central bank must make discretionary judgements on a case-by-case basis, and these judgements must shift frequently. Such a strategy, however, is not without its risks. Central banks have no particular advantage with respect to information on the transmission mechanism and on the structure of the economic and financial system. Therefore, in practice, their actions, too, are marked by uncertainty and an incomplete information set. When confronted with changes, the central bank has to decide whether these changes are permanent or transitory, real or nominal. In an information variable strategy, each change will be evaluated on a case-by-case basis by the central bank, and, depending on its judgment, induce a policy move. Since the rational public knows this strategy and knows that this evaluation will necessarily be based on imperfect information, uncertainty will increase, credibility will be at risk and policy plans are in danger of being time-inconsistent (Kydland and Prescott, 1977).

3 CO-MOVEMENTS IN LONG-TERM INTEREST RATES AND THE ROLE OF EXCHANGE RATE EXPECTATIONS: EVIDENCE FROM SURVEY DATA

3.1 Introduction

Developments in bond markets over the past several years, in particular the decrease in international yield spreads, have raised questions about the relations between long-term interest rates, globalisation of financial activities, and the exchange rate regime. It is generally accepted that under fixed exchange rates, globalisation of financial activities implies a high degree of convergence of long-term interest rates and synchronisation of their movements over time. Interest rates are determined by conditions in the fixed exchange rate region as a whole, rather than in individual countries, and there is correspondingly reduced scope for independent monetary policy by a single country.[1] Under floating exchange rates, interest rates differ across countries, in both real and nominal terms, because the existing pressures on financial markets are absorbed by movements in the countries' exchange rates or expected exchange rate developments. A rise in one country's interest rate relative to that of a partner is effectively offset by an expected future depreciation or a rise in the relative risk premium on its currency.

Notwithstanding the greater importance of long-term interest rates for the business cycle in most countries, the empirical literature on international interest rate linkages focussing on short-term assets generally outnumbers the studies using long-term rates.[2] This reflects the fact that financial instruments traded at the long end of the market generally lack a well-developed forward market. While it is true that forward markets are most developed at the three-month maturity and do not exist at maturities greater than two years, even among well-traded currencies, in the 1980s the currency swap market became sufficiently developed to hedge exchange rate risk for long-term investments as well (Popper, 1990, 1993, and Fletcher and Taylor, 1996). Like a forward contract, a currency swap allows a domestic investor to hold a foreign currency denominated asset

[1] Here we abstract from the exception to this rule that applies for the anchor country in a fixed but adjustable exchange rate regime like Bretton-Woods or the European Monetary System. An excellent description of this so-called 'n-1 problem' is provided by De Grauwe (1994).

[2] Recent studies involving long-term rates are Kasman and Pigott (1988), Howe and Pigott (1991), Pigott (1993), Throop (1994), and Fell (1996).

without currency risk.[3] Additional to the gradual worldwide abolition of capital controls, this financial innovation may have increased the linkage of international long-term interest rates.[4]

Financial innovations like currency swaps should contribute to an integration of international capital markets by increasing capital mobility. In this chapter we investigate whether this increased mobility led to a measurable increase in co-movement of national bond yields. This focus on long-term interest differentials is by itself an important contribution to the existing literature, which, as mentioned earlier, mainly concentrates on short-term instruments. The second contribution is that we use direct measures of exchange rate expectations, obtained from survey data, which allow us to directly assess the uncovered interest rate parity (UIP) relationship. Our hypothesis is that increases in international capital mobility may be expected to result in a greater likelihood of validating this UIP relationship, as, under these circumstances, the scope for interest rate arbitrage increases and the impact on interest rate differentials of factors other than (expected) exchange rate movements should steadily diminish. Empirical tests of UIP thus far have usually been combined with the rational expectations hypothesis, thereby allowing actual exchange rate movements to proxy for expected ones. The bulk of this evidence indicates not just that exchange rate changes fail to move one-for-one with interest rate differentials, but rather that these changes are substantial and in the *opposite* direction to that implied by UIP (McCallum, 1994). Froot (1990) has calculated an average estimated regression coefficient across some 75 published estimates of *minus* 0.88. A few estimates are positive, but all of them are distinctly smaller than the null hypothesis of a coefficient of +1.

This chapter is organised as follows. In the next section we present some stylized facts and briefly discuss the uncovered interest rate parity relation, followed, in section 3, by a description of the dataset used. Section 4 puts the theoretical predictions to an empirical test. Section 5 concludes.

3.2 Recent developments in international bond markets: a first look

Figure 1 displays the development of long-term (ten year) government bonds yields for the United States, Germany, France, United Kingdom, Switzerland, and Japan from 1981 onwards.[5] During the initial years after

---

[3] The term currency swap refers to a long-term 'cross-currency interest rate swap' that entails an exchange of payment streams.

[4] Deviations from a covered parity in interest rates appear to be somewhat larger among long-term assets than among short-term assets, but the differences are small for the major currencies (Popper, 1993; Fletcher and Taylor, 1996).

[5] We used the so-called benchmark bonds, obtained from the BIS-databank, for all countries.

the second oil crisis (1979), many countries experienced strong upward pressure on long-term interest rates, when inflation pressures rose and monetary policy was tightened quite aggressively. Since the early 1980s, bond yields have gradually come down and there has been a marked convergence of nominal (and also real) long-term interest rates among the larger countries (with the exception of Switzerland). This trend broadly corresponds to the declining trend in inflation during this period and the simultaneous reduction in inflation divergences across the major regions. In most countries, this process was interrupted in the periods surrounding the stock market collapse of 1987 and the Fed-tightening of 1994. With the benefit of hindsight, the causes of these bond market corrections are well known. In both phases, substantial concerns about the return of inflationary pressures in the US economy developed, and bond yields rose significantly.

Figure 3.1: Long-term government bond-yields

Per cent

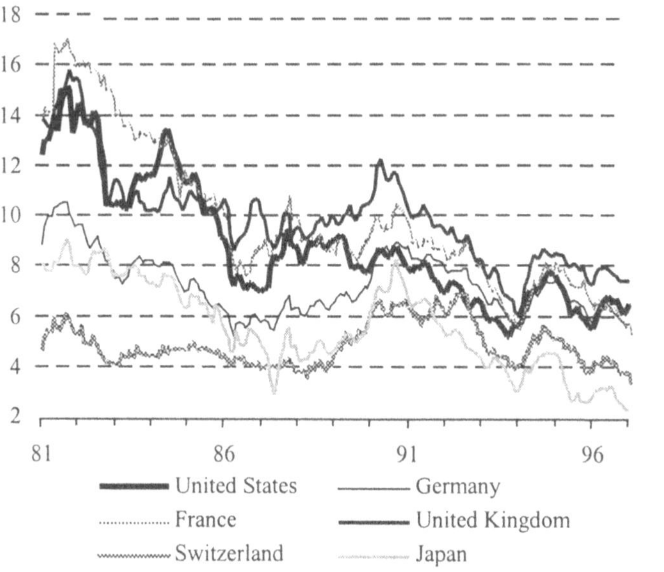

Table 3.1 documents the major swings which have taken place in international bond markets since the early 1980s in more detail.[6] Especially

It is important that the properties of these bond contracts are identical (so that they differ only in currency of denomination), and the benchmark bonds come closest to this ideal. It is however likely that differences remain, for example because of variations in the degree of liquidity of the underlying markets and differences in the method by which the contracts are sold (Holmes and Wu, 1997).

[6] The methodology which has been adopted to classify a major swing in the bond market is similar to that used by the NBER to date business cycles (Bry and Boschan, 1971). Peaks

during the 1980s, where changes in fundamentals can be seen, long-term interest rates accross the major countries have been pushed apart, often with accompanying movements in exchange rates. Countries that had experienced the largest inflation increases towards the end of the 1970s, such as the United States, the United Kingdom, and France, had to allow for higher bond yields than Germany and Japan around the turn of the decade, while their currencies generally fell vis-à-vis the Deutschemark and the yen. US long-term interest rates rose between spring-1983 and mid-1984 while at the same time interest rates in Europe and Japan were generally falling, due in part to the effects of US fiscal expansion in raising the demand for domestic savings relative to its supply. The pressures resulting from this divergence in long-term interest rates were also reflected in the sharp appreciation of the dollar in this period, as well as by the reversal of that appreciation that began in 1985 and occurred as US bond yields were falling back.

Table 3.1: Peak to trough analysis of major swings in international bond markets

Market	United States		Germany		France		United Kingdom		Switzerland		Japan	
type	Start	Change	Start	Change	Start	Change	Start	Change	Start	Change	Start	Change
bull	81/09	-494	81/09	-322	81/09	-928	81/10	-719	81/09	-191	81/09	-631
bear	83/05	+318	83/03	+96					83/01	+72		
bull	84/06	-648	83/12	-301					85/03	-117		
bear	87/01	+244	86/04	+367	86/08	+299	86/04	+204			87/05	+552
bull	87/10	-168			87/10	-239	86/11	-160				
bear	89/12	+105			89/08	+211	88/04	+314	88/04	+292		
bull	90/09	-356	90/10	-339	90/09	-481	90/04	-611	90/04	-264	90/09	-531
bear	93/10	+262	94/01	+194	94/01	+252	94/01	+257	93/12	+149	93/12	+160
bull	94/11	-230	95/01	-179	95/01	-244	94/09	-139	94/09	-164	94/10	-229
end	96/01		96/12		96/12		96/01		96/12		96/12	

Notes: Changes are measured in basis points. Peaks and troughs were identified using a 12-month moving window. A 'bull' market is defined as at least 6 consecutive months of declining bond yields and a 'bear' market is similarly defined for rising bond yields.

For the 1990s, however, Table 3.1 would seem to reveal a somewhat larger synchronisation among government bond yields than in the previous decade. Apart from the correction after the Fed-tightening of 1994, the 1990s have been characterised by declining bond yields world-wide. In view of the experience of the 1980s, it is the circumstances surrounding the

and troughs were identified using a 12-month moving window. A 'bull' market is defined as at least 6 consecutive months of declining bond yields and a 'bear' market is similarly defined.

interest rate developments, and not the mere fact that they moved together, that would seem somewhat unusual. The 1994 long-term interest rate run-ups in Europe and Japan followed a prolonged period of declining short-term interest rates and weak economic activity. The experience of the 1990s thus suggests that the degree to which long-term interest rates are free to vary with national conditions should not be overstated, even under floating exchange rates.[7] Globalisation of portfolio trading strategies may have led to a more profound influence of aggregate international conditions with resulting spillovers among markets.

Figure 3.2: Correlations of changes in domestic bond yields vis-à-vis the United States
Rolling 60-month periods

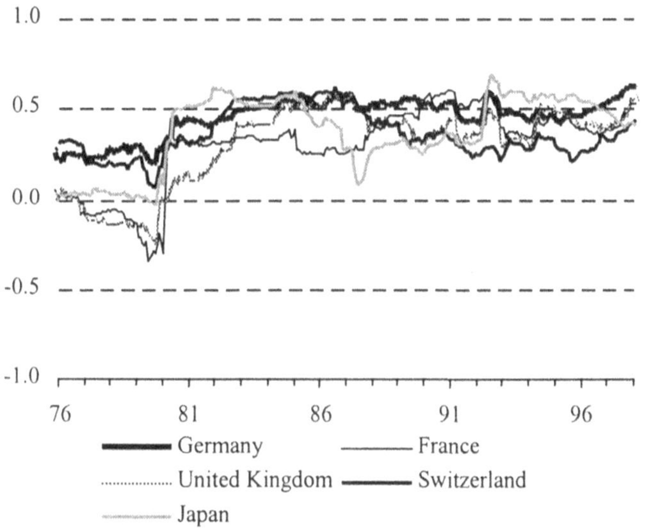

More formal evidence on the degree to which long-term interest rates have become more synchronised with globalisation can be extracted from bilateral correlations of their changes against those in the major market. In this respect, the US bond market is clearly the world's dominant market, with a size about three times that of Germany, for instance. For the five countries under investigation, figure 3.2 displays 5-year rolling correlations of monthly changes in domestic bond yields vis-à-vis US yields over the period 1976-1996. Apart from the stylized fact that co-movements in long-term interest rates among the major industrialised economies were stronger in the 1980s and 1990s than during the 1970s (see a.o. Frankel, 1989), by

[7] In this respect, Browne and Tease (1992) find little tendency for long-term interest rates to vary systematically with the business cycle.

this measure there seems to have been no systematic further increase in the bilateral synchronisations since the early 1980s. Furthermore, correlations have varied considerably over time. Although interest rates were indeed relatively highly correlated over the last few years (with the exception of Switzerland), generally they were not more so than in the 1980s.

Figure 3.3: Proportion of variance explained by the first four principal components of changes in bond yields
Rolling 60-month periods

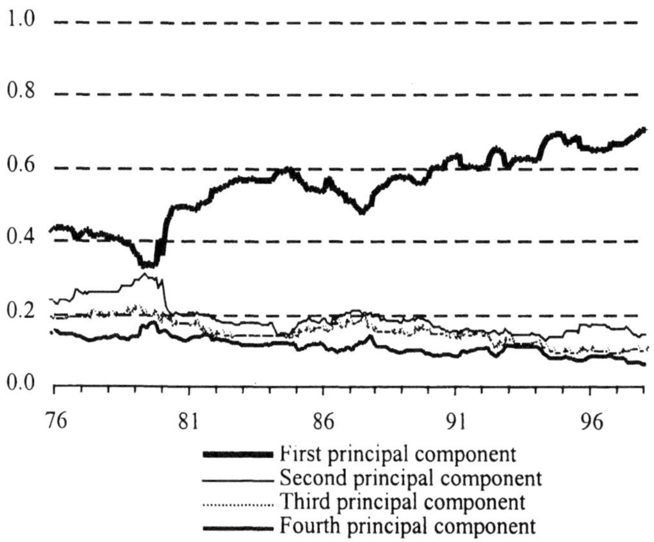

Finally, figure 3.3 looks into the co-movements in bond yields from a multilateral perspective, by depicting the proportion of variance among the various interest rates explained by the first four principal components of the changes in bond yields in all six countries under investigation. Following the suggestion of Gagnon and Unferth (1995), we interpret the first principal component, which is optimal in the sense that no other linear combination accounts for more of the total variance of the interest rates, as the 'world' interest rate. The more intense the capital market integration, the higher the correlations between the (changes in) interest rates and the greater the proportion of variance explained by the first component. Figure 3.3 would suggest that the international integration of bond markets did indeed increase since the mid-1980s, albeit gradually.[8]

All in all, the message from Figures 3.1-3.3 and Table 3.1 is rather

[8] Based on an analysis of twelve OECD-countries, Fase and Vlaar (1997) reach a similar conclusion.

mixed. This should not be too much of a surprise, since the analysis thus far has been confined to bond yields only, without any reference to contemporaneous developments in foreign exchange markets. As is well known, however, exchange rates among the largest industrialised countries have fluctuated quite substantially in the period under investigation. In the remainder of this chapter, we shall therefore introduce exchange rate movements into the analysis.

The effect of exchange rate movements on interest rate relations can be described in terms of the standard uncovered interest rate parity relation (UIP). Its most restrictive representation assumes risk neutral investors and perfect substitutability between assets that are comparable in all respects except their currency of denomination (Blundell-Wignall and Brown, 1991). Under these conditions, UIP states that the difference between any two countries' nominal interest rates equals the expected depreciation of the first country's currency against the second's (over the life of the instrument):

$$i(k)_t - i(k)_t^* = ({}_t s_{t+k}^e - s_t)/k \qquad (1)$$

where $i(k)_t$ denotes the nominal interest rate on a financial instrument with a remaining life of k periods in the home country, $i(k)_t^*$ its foreign equivalent and s_t the natural logarithm of the nominal exchange rate (domestic currency price of a foreign currency unit), all at time t. The (log of the) exchange rate at maturity as expected by investors at time t is denoted as ${}_t s_{t+k}^e$. Dropping the assumption of risk neutrality introduces risk premia in equation (1). Market participants for example know that the exchange rate is unlikely to be predicted with much adequacy. Being risk-averse, they expect to be compensated for this uncertainty if they are to be induced to buy the foreign-currency denominated asset. The possibility that future capital movements could be reduced by political measures also introduces an element of uncertainty, for which the risk averse investor may command a premium. These and possible other risk factors are reflected in our analysis by an *ex hypothesi* constant risk premium on the k-period bond in the home country, denoted as σ. Expected exchange rate movements and a risk premium are the two major factors which drive a wedge between domestic and foreign currency nominal interest rates on comparable assets (Christiansen and Pigott, 1997):

$$i(k)_t - i(k)_t^* = ({}_t s_{t+k}^e - s_t)/k + \sigma \qquad (2)$$

The empirical counterpart of equation (2) is as follows:

$$i(k)_t - i(k)_t^* = \alpha + \beta\left({}_t s_{t+k}^e - s_t\right)/k + \varepsilon_t \tag{3}$$

were ε(*t*) represents a disturbance term, the properties of which will be discussed in a next section. In general, only the interest rates are observable in equation (3). As this causes identification problems, we propose to use direct observations on exchange rate expectations obtained from surveys among market participants.

3.3 Survey data and methodology

The principal benefit of using survey data is that one obtains a direct measure of agents' beliefs that is immune to errors introduced by exchange risk premia, thus allowing for a direct test of the interaction between exchange rate expectations and the determination of interest rates or interest differentials (Frankel and Froot, 1987). Especially in the case of exchange rate expectations, the respondents to the surveys often participate directly in the spot and forward exchange markets, where they have up-to-the-minute information on the values of the currencies involved. Furthermore, the widespread econometric practice of inferring from *ex post* data what investors must have expected also tends to give misleading answers (Froot and Frankel, 1989). Critics of these survey data, however, typically question the extent to which such data are representative for 'the market'. If we follow the literature in talking as if there exists a single expectation that is homogeneously held by all investors that we measure by the median survey response, it is by definition measured with error.

In this chapter, the data come from two different surveys: one conducted by Business International Corporation over the period 1985 to 1992, and one conducted by Consensus Forecasts over the period 1989 to present. From 1985 to 1992, Business International Corporation has been conducting a monthly survey of exchange rate expectations covering ten currencies relative to the dollar and eight currencies relative to the Deutschemark. For publication purposes, some 30-odd treasurers of multinationals and private banks are asked a few days prior to month's end to fax three-, six-, and twelve-month ahead expectations of a number of currencies with projections being made from the beginning of the following month. The dates on which the surveys were conducted have been recorded as well as the spot and forward rates recorded on that particular day. In Cavaglia, Verschoor, and Wolff (1993), and Cavaglia and Wolff (1996), these forecasts are described and evaluated in more detail. Likewise, every month from October 1989 onwards, Consensus Forecasts has surveyed over

200 prominent financial and economic forecasters about their estimates of a range of variables, including future growth, inflation, interest rates, and exchange rates. More than 30 countries are covered and the reference data, together with analyses and polls on topical issues, are published in a monthly bulletin. Currency forecasts are documented at three- and twelve-month horizons.

Unfortunately, the bond yields under investigation correspond with a term to maturity of approximately ten years, whereas the maximum horizon at which exchange rate forecasts are available is confined to one year. To overcome this problem, two alternative approaches will be considered. In the first approach, we formulate two extreme assumptions regarding the expectations formation beyond the one year horizon, which enable us to set some plausible bounds to the coefficient of the expected depreciation in the UIP relationship (β in equation (3)). Since a closer inspection of the three-, six-, and twelve-month forecasts revealed that the expected percentage of depreciation varies almost linearly with the horizon of the forecast, the one-year ahead forecast may well serve as a proxy for the *annualised* ten-year ahead forecast (that is the expected *rate* of depreciation). This assumption amounts to a linear extrapolation of the one-year forecast to the ten-year horizon, which could be regarded as one extreme way of modelling investors' expectations. On the other hand, the observation that survey forecasts are available only up to a one-year horizon could be taken as an illustration of the fact that investors' expectations simply do not extent beyond this horizon. In that case, the one-year-ahead forecast would also apply to the entire maturity of ten years, so that the expected rate of depreciation over the whole time span is ten times smaller than in the first case. It is conceivable that the 'true' expected rate of depreciation over the ten-year horizon will lie in between both extremes, so that the estimated coefficients can be interpreted as lower and upper bounds. To check this claim, the second approach consists of re-estimating our UIP equations for twelve-month Euromarket interest rate differentials, where the term precisely matches the forecast horizon.

In the previous section we derived an expression for the nominal bond yield differential in terms of the expected depreciation and a risk premium (equation (3)). Table 3.2 presents time series evidence for their empirical counterparts, given the direct observations on exchange rate forecasts described above. The expected rate of depreciation is proxied here by the one-year ahead survey forecasts. For the entire sample, spanning the period December 1985-January 1997 and comprising both the Business International and the Consensus forecasts, the results of the unit root tests seem clear-cut: bond yield differentials, expected depreciation and risk premia are by and large all stationary.[9] However, for the subsamples, especially the Business International period, the unit root tests provide inconsistent results. For example, for all five countries the null of nonstationarity could not be rejected for the long-run interest rate differential. However, this differential is a linear combination of variables for which this null is clearly rejected (i.e. the expected depreciation and the risk premium). This inconsistency is an illustration of the low power of unit root tests (in this case the augmented Dickey-Fuller tests) against stationary alternatives in small samples (Campbell and Perron, 1991). This is especially true when the series under investigation are near-integrated processes.

Table 3.2: Testing for nonstationarity: augmented Dickey-Fuller tests

	Germany	France	United Kingdom	Switzerland	Japan
A. Entire sample: 1985:12-1997:01 (N=134)					
long run interest	-1.97*	-2.04*	-3.15*	-1.25	-0.49
differential vs US	I(0)	I(0)	I(0)	I(1)	I(1)
Expected	-2.35*	-3.73**	-4.08**	-2.35*	-2.43*
depreciation	I(0)	I(0)	I(0)	I(0)	I(0)
risk	-3.46*	-3.91**	-2.61**	-3.18*	-1.96*
premium	I(0)	I(0)	I(0)	I(0)	I(0)
B. Business International: 1985:12-1992:01 (N=74)					
long run interest					
differential vs US	-1.48	-1.54	-2.29	-2.23	-0.96
	I(1)	I(1)	I(1)	I(1)	I(1)
Expected	-2.80*	-3.85**	-4.82**	-3.04**	-3.64**
depreciation	I(0)	I(0)	I(0)	I(0)	I(0)
risk	-4.07**	-4.72**	-6.36**	-4.12**	-4.29**
premium	I(0)	I(0)	I(0)	I(0)	I(0)
C. Consensus Forecast: 1989:10-1997:01 (N=88)					
long run interest					
differential vs US	-3.63*	-2.86	-3.65*	-0.78	-4.29**
	I(0)	I(1)	I(0)	I(1)	I(0)
Expected	-3.01*	-3.04*	-2.98*	-2.94*	-2.04*
depreciation	I(0)	I(0)	I(0)	I(0)	I(0)
risk	-3.36**	-3.73**	-3.67*	-3.03*	-1.59
premium	I(0)	I(0)	I(0)	I(0)	I(1)

Note: ** (*) indicates significance at 1% (5%). Constant and linear time trend included when significant. Number of lagged differences chosen as to render the residual white noise.

[9] In composing the entire sample, we discarded the observations from the Business International survey for the period that coincided with the available data from the Consensus forecast. As both datasets appeared to be very similar for the overlapping period, discarding the Consensus data would not have changed our conclusions.

Failure to reject the unit-root hypothesis might thus be a result of the power deficiency of the standard tests rather than being evidence against stationarity of the series themselves. We investigated two possible causes of the power deficiency, i.e. the specific construction of the standard tests and the lack of obervations. We focus the discussion on interest rate differentials, since the outcomes of the standard tests for the expected depreciation and risk premium consistently point in the same direction (of stationarity).

The null hypothesis under the standard unit root tests is of nonstationarity, and this construction ensures that the null of a unit root will be accepted unless there is strong evidence against it. This prompted the use of the Kwiatkowski et al. (KPSS, 1992) method, where the null is of stationarity and the alternative of a unit root. As the test is widely used, we will only briefly discuss it here. KPSS (1992) propose a test of the null hypothesis that an observable series is stationary around a deterministic trend. The series is expressed as the sum of deterministic trend, random walk and stationary error, and the test is the LM-test of the hypothesis that the random walk has zero variance. We performed two KPSS-tests, one on

Table 3.3: Testing for stationarity of the interest rate differential: KPSS test

	Germany	France	United Kingdom	Switzerland	Japan
A. Entire sample: 1985:12-1997:01 (N=134)					
η_τ	0.19*	0.11	0.10	0.17*	0.18*
	I(1)	I(0)	I(0)	I(1)	I(1)
η_μ	0.81*	0.14	0.12	0.68*	0.20
	I(1)	I(0)	I(0)	I(1)	I(0)
B. Business International: 1985:12-1992:01 (N=74)					
η_τ	0.17*	0.12	0.10	0.17*	0.16*
	I(1)	I(0)	I(0)	I(1)	I(1)
η_μ	0.71*	0.17	0.25	0.56*	0.42
	I(1)	I(0)	I(0)	I(1)	I(0)
C. Consensus Forecast: 1989:10-1997:01 (N=88)					
η_τ	0.17*	0.06	0.13	0.17*	0.14
	I(1)	I(0)	I(0)	I(1)	I(0)
η_μ	0.25	0.51*	0.78*	0.21	0.80*
	I(0)	I(1)	I(1)	I(0)	I(1)

Note: * indicates significance at 5%. Critical values for η_τ and η_μ at the 5% significance level, obtained from KPSS (1992), are 0.146 and 0.463, respectively.

the OLS residuals of a regression of the interest rate differential on an intercept and time trend (η_τ) and another on the residuals of a regression of the differential on an intercept (η_μ). The Bartlett window used in the construction of the denominator of the KPSS-statistic has lag length $T^{0.5}$, as suggested by KPSS (1992). The results are reported in Table 3.3. The null hypothesis is that the interest rate differential is stationary. The results are qualitatively similar to those reported in table 3.2, in that the evidence is mixed.[10] In some cases the value of the test statistic exceeds the critical value (as reported in KPSS,1992), rejecting the null of stationarity in favour of the alternative of non-stationarity, in other cases the null is accepted. We conclude that the KPSS tests do not resolve the inconsistency.

A different route to address this problem follows the suggestion of Wu (1996) and Wu and Zhang (1996). They considered a panel of cross-country interest rate differential series as a system of autoregressive processes and employed the multivariate estimation procedure developed by Abuaf and Jorion (1990). The latter suggest pooling the data and estimate the following system of equations using seemingly unrelated regressions (SUR):[11]

$$x_{i,t} = \alpha_i + \delta_i t + \beta x_{i,t-1} + \sum_{j=1}^{k} \varphi_{i,j} \Delta x_{t-j} + \varepsilon_{t,i} \tag{4}$$

where x denotes the long run interest rate differential, i=Germany, France, the United Kingdom, Switzerland, and Japan and t=1,2,...,T. Equation (4) can be interpreted as the multivariate analogue of the augmented Dickey-Fuller equation, allowing for an intercept and linear time trend in the deterministic part of the process. The lagged terms of the differences are included to correct for possible serial correlations.[12] The test for the null hypothesis of $\beta=1$ is based on the statistic $\hat{t}=(\hat{\beta}-1)/s(\hat{\beta})$, where $\hat{\beta}$ is the SUR-estimate and $s(\hat{\beta})$ its estimated standard error. As the distribution of

[10] Note that for some individual countries, the results between standard and KPSS unit root tests differ, adding to the confusion.

[11] Using this procedure implies a power gain *vis-à-vis* single equation estimation as in table 2 for at least two reasons. First, SUR utilizes the cross-sectional variations of interest rate differentials as additional information in estimation and testing, which is ignored in the single-equation framework. There exists considerable cross-sectional correlation between movements in interest rates (strongest between Switzerland and Germany (0.81), followed by France-Germany (0.74)). Second, under the null hypothesis of a unit root in all interest rate differentials, this unit root should be imposed on all countries simultaneously. As table 4 below indicates, the restriction that $\beta_i = \beta \; \forall i$ cannot be rejected at conventional significance levels for our panel of countries. Accordingly, Monte Carlo simulations performed by Wu and Zhang (1996) revealed that the multivariate Dickey-Fuller test has substantially higher power than standard ADF tests.

[12] In table 4, the results are presented for k=0, as no lagged differences were significant. We re-estimated the model with various values of k and obtained similar results.

this statistic $\hat{t}$ is unknown for a system of equations, we generated critical values using Monte Carlo simulations, as in Fuller (1976). The simulation is conducted as follows. The data generation process is based on a first-order autoregressive process, with parameter equal to unity and without a drift. The sample size T is chosen to correspond to our specific sample size (74 observations for the Business International data and 88 for the Consensus Forecast data). In each experiment, we generated 5 innovations from a multivariate normal distribution with mean zero and a given covariance matrix. This matrix is estimated by the cross-correlations of the residuals obtained from regressions of the first differences of interest rates on their significant own lagged terms.[13] These random innovations and the data generation process described enable us to generate five unit root processes of T observations each. These simulated observations are used to estimate the five-equation system (4) by SUR. We next calculated the value of the test statistic t.

Table 3.4: SUR estimation of pooled interest rate differentials

Variable	*Business International: Pooled # observations: 365*	*Consensus Forecast: Pooled # observations: 435*
Intercept Germany	-0.33	0.18
	(3.20)	(2.93)
Intercept France	0.03	0.32
	(0.44)	(4.02)
Intercept United Kingdom	0.19	0.49
	(1.74)	(4.59)
Intercept Switzerland	-0.64	-0.17
	(4.24)	(2.22)
Intercept Japan	-0.54	-0.08
	(3.71)	(1.24)
$\beta_i = \beta$: χ^2-test	1.63	2.08
(p-value)	(0.80)	(0.08)
β	-0.14	-0.16
	(5.14)	(6.64)*

Notes: The model consists of a regression of the first-differences of the interest rate differential on a country-specific intercept, the lagged interest rate differential and a country specific linear time trend (not reported). Lagged differences of the interest rate differential were found not to be significant. i= Germany, France, United Kingdom, Switzerland, and Japan. Absolute t-values are in parentheses unless indicated otherwise. * indicates significance at 5%. The 5% critical values pertaining to the absolute t-statistic for β for the Business International and Consensus Forecast periods are 6.32 and 6.28, respectively. These are based on ten thousand Monte Carlo replications under the null hypothesis that the process is a random walk without drift.

[13] The Monte Carlo distribution is robust to alternative specifications of the innovation covariance matrix, see Abuaf and Jorion (1990).

This experiment was repeated 10.000 times to generate the empircal distribution of the test statistic under the null hypothesis of $\beta = 1$. We calculated from this distribution the 5% critical values. As can be seen from Table 4, the null of nonstationarity is rejected only for the Consensus Forecast period.

We conclude from the analyses presented in Tables 3.3 and 3.4 that different methods do not seem to provide a definitive answer regarding the stationarity of the interest rate differentials. UIP predicts a linear relationship between interest rate differentials at the one hand, and expected depreciations and risk premia on the other. Since the data clearly indicate that the latter variables are stationary throughout, we proceed presuming that interest rate differentials are also stationary.

3.4 Empirical results

In this section we test for uncovered interest rate parity *vis-à-vis* the US, regressing the long-term interest rate differential with the US for the UK, Germany, France, Japan and Switzerland on an intercept, and the expected rate of depreciation of the US dollar in these latter countries. In addition to its interpretation of a risk premium (see section 3.2), the intercept is included to take into account a number of country-specific characteristics of the financial system that are less time-varying, such as for instance the liquidity of the US bond markets *vis-à-vis* those in the other countries or the fiscal climate (McCallum, 1994). Since the advent of new financial instruments and the abolition of capital controls increased long-term capital mobility, our hypothesis is that in the more recent sample, covered by the Consensus Forecasts, there should be stronger evidence in favour of UIP than in the earlier sample, covered by Business International. Table 5 presents the results of the regressions described above, using OLS but with an adjustment of the covariance matrix as suggested by Newey and West (1987).[14] Upon investigating table 3.5, three features stand out. First, although most of the coefficients of the expected rate of depreciation have the expected (positive) sign, for none of the subsamples (and neither for the entire sample) are the coefficients near unity, as would be implied by strict

[14] This correction is necessary because the forecast horizon implicit in the expected depreciation (12 months) exceeds the sampling interval (1 month), implying the so-called 'overlapping observations' problem. The error term is serially correlated (more specifically, it follows a MA(11) process), thereby rendering the OLS estimates of the covariance matrix inconsistent, despite consistent parameter estimates (Hansen and Hodrick, 1980; Frankel and Froot, 1987;Chinn and Frankel, 1994). The Newey-West standard errors are asymptotically consistent in the presence of serial correlation as well as heteroskedasticity (Hamilton, 1994).

Table 3.5: Testing for uncovered interest rate parity
model : interest differential= intercept + expected depreciation

	Germany	France	United Kingdom	Switzerland	Japan
A. Entire sample: 1985:12-1997:01 (N=134)					
Intercept	-0.81	0.49	1.75	-3.01	-2.73
	(4.25)	(3.59)	(8.82)	(13.37)	(13.20)
exp depreciation	0.18	0.09	0.01	0.17	0.00
	(7.20)	(3.57)	(0.28)	(5.81)	(0.13)
B. Business International: 1985:12-1992:01 (N=74)					
Intercept	-1.29	0.58	1.59	-3.48	-2.77
	(6.76)	(5.62)	(5.85)	(15.00)	(10.26)
exp depreciation	0.19	0.11	0.11	0.18	0.11
	(7.22)	(6.38)	(2.13)	(5.07)	(2.04)
C. Consensus Forecast: 1989:10-1997:01 (N=88)					
Intercept	0.02	0.51	1.94	-2.09	-2.24
	(0.16)	(2.16)	(9.58)	(18.70)	(11.08)
exp depreciation	0.08	0.09	-0.00	0.08	-0.04
	(4.00)	(2.13)	(0.19)	(2.94)	(1.13)

Note: absolute *t*-values, computed with Newey-West standard errors, are in parentheses.

UIP. However, one should keep in mind that underlying Table 3.5 is the (rather extreme) assumption that the one-year ahead forecast can be extrapolated to the ten year horizon linearly. The estimates of Table 3.5 can therefore be interpreted as the lower bound values of the 'true' coefficients. For instance, if we were to adhere to the other extreme assumption of a flat expectation beyond the one year horizon, the coefficients of the expected rate of depreciation would have to be multiplied by ten (*t*-statistics remain unaltered), so that some of them would even exceed unity. Second, there is no tendency for the coefficients of the expected rate of depreciation to increase from the first (that is early) to the second, recent, subsample. If anything, they are *de*creasing. The data therefore seem to reject the notion of increasing UIP-validation over time. Finally, despite the greater liquidity of the US bond markets, a number of intercepts are consistently negative and substantial, especially for Switzerland and Japan. Compared to the other countries, both Switzerland and Japan are characterised by a relatively closed and to some extent also protected financial system, which may be have kept domestic bond yields artificially low.[15]

It could also be argued that liberalisation and integration of capital markets manifest themselves primarily in an increased interwovenness of *all* six bond markets under investigation. In this case a multivariate procedure which exploits cross-sectional information on variations in

[15] Moreover, the attractive fiscal regime in Switzerland seems relevant in explaining the different results for that country.

expected exchange rates and interest rate differentials would be better equipped to deal with UIP than the single-equation framework applied in Table 3.5. Table 3.6 presents the results of a regression analysis, using the SUR technique, on a dataset consisting of a pool of data on the five individual countries *vis-à-vis* the US. The results presented in Table 3.6 indicate that the conclusion derived from Table 3.5 remains the same: the parameter estimates of the coefficient of the expected rate of depreciation show no discernable tendency to increase between both subsamples. Moreover, the estimates are generally even lower than in the bivariate equations, although their interpretation should again be restricted to that of a lower bound value. In addition, the hypothesis that the effects of an expected depreciation on the interest rate differential *vis-à-vis* the US are

Table 3.6: SUR estimation of pooled interest rate parity

	Germany	France	United Kingdom	Switzerland	Japan
A. Entire sample: 1985:12-1997:01 (pooled number of observations=664)					
Intercept	-0.67	0.52	1.76	-2.88	-2.75
	(8.00)	(8.36)	(21.15)	(30.18)	(30.56)
exp depreciation	0.11	0.08	0.00	0.12	0.03
	(7.87)	(6.88)	(0.34)	(8.76)	(2.61)
Hypothesis: coefficient of expected depreciation equal across countries					
$\chi^2 = 64.5$ (prob = 0.00), rejected					
B. Business International: 1985:12-1992:01 (pooled number of observations=370)					
Intercept	-1.14	0.63	1.86	-3.36	-2.76
	(10.17)	(10.09)	(13.15)	(27.19)	(19.33)
exp depreciation	0.09	0.09	0.03	0.10	0.06
	(5.55)	(6.90)	(1.11)	(5.01)	(2.14)
Hypothesis: coefficient of expected depreciation equal across countries					
$\chi^2 = 5.89$ (prob = 0.21), accepted					
estimated coefficient:	0.08				
	(7.43)				
C. Consensus Forecast: 1989:10-1997:01 (pooled number of observations=434)					
Intercept	0.05	0.53	1.89	-2.12	-2.30
	(0.48)	(5.82)	(19.52)	(25.92)	(25.02)
exp depreciation	0.07	0.09	0.01	0.08	0.00
	(8.09)	(6.56)	(0.82)	(7.13)	(0.21)
Hypothesis: coefficient of expected depreciation equal across countries					
$\chi^2 = 45.15$ (prob = 0.00), rejected					

Notes: The model regresses the interest rate differential on an intercept and the expected depreciation. Absolute *t*-values are in parentheses.

equal across countries is rejected for the Consensus subsample, in contrast to the earlier subsample. Although no formal test, this is surely counterintuitive 'evidence' against an increase in international co-movement on bond markets in recent years. In order to check our claim that the estimates of Tables 3.5 and 3.6 represent the lower bound of the 'true' parameter, Table 3.7 presents additional estimates of the UIP equations using twelve-month interest rate differentials instead of ten year bond yield differentials, again individually (OLS) as well as collectively (SUR).

Table 3.7: Testing for UIP using twelve-month interest rate differentials
model : interest differential= intercept + expected depreciation

	Germany	France	United Kingdom	Switzerland	Japan
A.1 Entire sample: 1985:12-1997:01 (N=134), OLS					
Intercept	-1.27	0.53	2.94	-2.05	-2.45
	(3.28)	(1.58)	(6.70)	(4.64)	(6.32)
Exp depreciation	0.41	0.35	0.04	0.22	0.02
	(5.00)	(4.62)	(0.49)	(2.94)	(0.30)
A.2 Entire sample: 1985:12-1997:01 (N=664), SUR					
Intercept	-1.00	0.71	3.06	-1.94	-2.50
	(3.86)	(5.76)	(16.65)	(8.52)	(14.17)
Exp depreciation	0.29	0.29	0.00	0.18	0.09
	(9.77)	(11.06)	(0.08)	(8.16)	(4.18)
B.1 Business International: 1985:12-1992:01 (N=74), OLS					
Intercept	-1.75	1.05	3.31	-2.29	-2.12
	(4.06)	(3.45)	(8.38)	(5.14)	(5.93)
exp depreciation	0.37	0.23	0.21	0.32	0.27
	(5.38)	(4.31)	(2.34)	(4.72)	(3.33)
B.2 Business International: 1985:12-1992:01 (N=370), SUR					
Intercept	-1.43	1.19	3.64	-2.08	-2.11
	(5.62)	(7.01)	(15.20)	(8.56)	(11.04)
exp depreciation	0.16	0.17	0.11	0.17	0.22
	(4.62)	(5.54)	(2.27)	(5.20)	(5.71)
C.1 Consensus Forecast: 1989:10-1997:01 (N=88),OLS					
Intercept	-0.22	0.36	2.87	-0.74	-1.93
	(0.45)	(0.58)	(0.53)	(1.24)	(3.92)
exp depreciation	0.34	0.41	0.06	0.11	-0.06
	(3.29)	(3.84)	(0.53)	(0.99)	(0.66)
C.2 Consensus Forecast: 1989:10-1997:01 (N=434), SUR					
Intercept	0.09	0.76	3.00	-0.89	-2.04
	(0.66)	(1.02)	(8.11)	(2.02)	(7.72)
exp depreciation	0.25	0.30	0.02	0.14	0.02
	(8.86)	(9.43)	(0.53)	(5.96)	(1.07)

Note: absolute *t*- values, in the OLS case computed with Newey-West standard errors, are in parentheses.

Strictly speaking, this exercise does not yield any new insight into the process of expectations formation beyond the one year horizon, but it does alleviate the mismatch between the forecast horizon and the term of the investment. Since the coefficients of the expected rate of depreciation are systematically higher than the corresponding estimates of Tables 3.5 and 3.6, Table 3.7 would seem to support our intuition that a linear extrapolation of the one-year ahead forecasts overestimates the 'true' expected rate of depreciation over the entire ten year horizon and, consequently, tends to introduce a downward bias in its UIP coefficient. On the other hand, a rough inspection of tables 3.5-3.7 indicates that most coefficients approximately double in magnitude, which is much less than the presumed tenfold increase under the alternative assumption of a flat exchange rate expectation beyond the one year horizon. This would tentatively suggest that a linear extrapolation is closer to the 'true' expected rate of depreciation than a flat extrapolation.

All in all, it would be at least one step too far to conclude that our evidence supports the validity of UIP among the 'industrialised' currencies. Nevertheless, it appears that exchange rates are consistently *expected* to move in the same direction as implied by UIP, albeit less than one-for-one.

Table 3.8: Granger causality tests

	Germany	France	United Kingdom	Switzerland	Japan
A. Entire sample: 1985:12-1997:01 (N=134)					
$H_0: r_f$ does not cause r_d	4.82*	4.70*	0.79	0.83	1.72
$H_0: r_d$ does not cause r_f	0.60	0.10	0.10	0.10	0.77
B. Business International: 1985:12-1992:01 (N=74)					
$H_0: r_f$ does not cause r_d	6.77*	2.76	0.31	0.32	0.95
$H_0: r_d$ does not cause r_f	2.56	0.3	0.37	0.68	2.06
C. Consensus Forecast: 1989:10-1997:01 (N=88)					
$H_0: r_f$ does not cause r_d	1.95	3.57	0.53	0.0	0.41
$H_0: r_d$ does not cause r_f	0.11	0.00	1.04	0.00	3.55

Notes: The model for the difference of the domestic (US) rate includes the difference of the US (domestic) interest rate and the expected depreciation.The explanatory variables are lagged one period; other lags were not significant. * indicates significant at 5%. r_f =US rate; r_d =domestic rate.

In this respect, our strategy of employing survey data instead of ex-post realisations to proxy for (unobservable) exchange rate expectations constitutes a clear improvement over the various studies summarised in Froot (1990) and McCallum (1994). Presumably, the improvement is due to the rejection of the combined hypothesis of rational expectations underlying these studies. It has often been documented that participants in the foreign exchange market do make systematic forecast errors and do not always use all information efficiently when forecasting (Frankel and Froot, 1987, Cavaglia, Verschoor, and Wolff, 1993, and Sobiechowski, 1996). Thus far, we have only studied the correlations between the various interest rates and the expected rate of depreciation by testing equation (3). However, correlation does not necessarily mean causation. To conclude our empirical analysis, Table 3.8 therefore presents the results of Granger-causality tests on bond yields. It is frequently asserted in the popular press that the dominance of the US bond market in terms of size extends to bond yields, in that the US bond yield leads the bond yields in other countries. The US bond yield is said to Granger-cause a domestic bond yield when movements in the former contribute significantly to the explanation of the latter, over-and-above lagged differences of the domestic bond yield and the expected movement of the exchange rate. It follows from Table 8 that, for the entire sample, the null hypothesis of no causality is rejected only for Germany and France. For most of the subsamples, there does not seem to be any convincing evidence pointing towards a particular direction of causality. This is in particular the case for the most recent subsample, the Consensus Forecast period. This finding may be due to the frquency of the data. Christiansen and Pigott (1997), using daily observations, find somewhat clearer patterns of causality.

3.5 Concluding remarks

Empirical tests of the uncovered parity relationship traditionally used short-term interest rates, because until the mid 1980s no financial instruments existed that enabled market participants to hedge for long-term interest rate positions. This situation changed in the latter part of the 1980s, when cross-currency interest rate swaps created the possibility of hedging long-term currency positions (Popper, 1993). Interest arbitrage conditions which previously applied only to short-term assets now enables long-term financial capital to become international mobile across distinct bond markets. This chapter has investigated the uncovered interest rate parity relationship between bond yield differentials vis-à-vis the US for the UK, Germany, France, Japan and Switzerland with the aid of directly observed exchange rate expectations against the US dollar derived from survey data. Globalisation and integration of international financial markets should imply a stronger tendency towards co-movement of financial variables, such as bond yields. Our empirical analysis distinguished between bilateral and multilateral co-movements of bond yields. Although a quick visual inspection of major swings in international bond markets would suggest otherwise, we could not find empirical evidence supporting the notion of increased co-movement since the early 1980s. Nevertheless, the results of the UIP tests suggested that our strategy of employing survey data instead of ex-post realisations to proxy for (unobservable) exchange rate expectations constitutes a clear improvement over the existing literature.

There are various explanations of our findings. First and foremost, the variant of the UIP relationship which we used assumed constant risk premia. The empirical rejection of this relationship could therefore be an indication of the inappropriateness of this assumption. Secondly, when projecting the UIP relationship on bond yields, we implicitly assumed that the relationship between the bond market and the currency markets was as tight as the relationship between money markets and currency markets. Our results are an indication that this is not the case, and seem to warrant further (theoretical) research on the links between bond and currency markets. Thirdly, observed deviations from UIP may also be due to factors as transaction costs, non-comparability of assets and measurement error (Popper, 1993). From a policy perspective, the main implication of our work is that national factors still exert an important influence on bond yields. This does not necessarily make things easier for the policy maker, since the relationship between long-term interest rates and the variables under direct control of the central bank may be equally blurred.

4 INTERNATIONAL INTERDEPENDENCE OF BUSINESS CYCLES: THE USE OF LEADING INDICATORS FOR FORECASING AND ANALYSIS [1]

4.1 Introduction

One of the most striking aspects of the business cycle is that it is a phenomenon which, sooner or later, is reflected in similar patterns in almost every macroeconomic variable, thus illustrating their interdependence. Such interdependence is not restricted to national macroeconomic variables either; it is also a global phenomenon. The world's economies are strongly integrated. At a national level, the cyclical movements of some economic variables are known to begin earlier than most of the others, because these variables themselves cause the economic tide to turn, or because they detect the ebb and flow at an early stage, or because they are quick to respond to other leading time series. Similarly, at an international level, it is known that the business cycle of some countries leads that of others, implying that the leading country acts as the engine of growth.

Leading indicators are time series which lead the general business cycle and thus enable cyclical movements to be predicted. Various leading variables for a particular country can be combined into a single leading business cycle index. The use of composite leading indicators has a long and successful tradition dating back to 1919, when the American Professor Persons at Harvard University launched an *index of speculation* based on three price variables coupled with the index of share prices as a proxy of expectations. His work was continued by researchers at the National Bureau of Economic Research (NBER), founded in 1920, who went on to expand this method (Burns and Mitchell, 1938, 1946; Moore, 1961, 1975; Lahiri and Moore, 1991; Zarnowitz, 1991, 1992; see for a summary: Granger, 1980). The NBER method is used in almost every industrialized country. In many countries, monthly indicators are published which attract considerable interest. Its use involving the simultaneous calculation of leading indicators for more than one country is less common: examples are EC (1982), Klein and Moore (1983, 1985) and OECD (1987).

This chapter aims to develop and analyse leading indicators for

---

[1] Reprinted from *Journal of Forecasting*, 14 (1), (1995), J.M. Berk and J.A. Bikker, "International Interdependence of Business Cycles in the Manufacturing Industry: The Use of Leading indicators for Forecasting and Analysis", 1-23 .© 1995 with kind permission from John Wiley and Sons ltd, Chichester.

fifteen industrialized countries, using an improved variant of the NBER-method, based on Fase and Bikker (1985) and Bikker and De Haan (1988). This method is closest to that of the OECD, but differs from it in important respects. Unlike the OECD method, the present method takes account of the differences in the degree to which the basic component indicators lead the overall business cycle. In addition, the cyclical component calculated by us is less distorted by erratic movements, so that the turning points are much more clearly defined. The international interdependence of business cycles has been assessed by analysing the cyclical fluctuations of the various countries, measured by the reference indices introduced below. The business cycle interrelationships between countries can be exploited to improve the contructed national leading indicators and further enhance their predictive power.

The chapter is organised as follows. The next section explains how business cycles are measured. The method used for constructing the composite leading indicators is discussed in the third section. After a description of the data and the countries included, in the fourth section, the fifth section goes on to discuss the empirical results for the various leading indicators and accompanying reference indices. The sixth section looks at the international interdependence of business cycles. The seventh section describes how this interdependence can be utilized to improve the forecasting power of the national leading indicators. The chapter then ends with conclusions.

4.2 Measuring business cycles

As the components of time series of economic variables, (e.g. trend, business cycle, season, and random factors) are not observed, they are in fact determined by the method of decomposition used. The business cycle in the present study is a fluctuation in the level of economic activity over a period of at least two and not more than seven years, and is expressed in terms of the departure from a trend, referred to as the *deviation cycle*. Such a cycle is found by elimination of the seasonal component, the trend, and random factors. The seasonal component is filtered out with the X-11 procedure developed by the US Bureau of the Census. Census X-11 is widely used, mainly because of its wide applicability and the flexibility with which shifts in the seasonal pattern can be described.[2] Den Butter and Fase (1991) show that Census X-11 performs better than other mechanical methods and almost as good as methods based on ARIMA-models.

[2] Although heuristic by nature, Census X-11 is not entirely without a theoretical foundation. It can be shown that, in its reduced form, Census X-11 is based on a (close approximation of a) special case of a structural time series model (Den Butter and Mourik, 1990).

Structural time series models and causal models are good alternatives in principle but are less suitable for large-scale application, as in the present case, due to the laborious judgemental elements involved. (Incidentally, the choice of the seasonal adjustment method appears hardly to affect the calculations of the business cycle). A further motivation for using Census X-11 is the requirement of comparability with US data, as some important series were available only in seasonally adjusted form.

In eliminating the trend we acknowledge the criticism of Zarnowitz (1992, p. 212), who concluded that, on the whole, most trend models produce good approximations over limited periods only, but lack the flexibility required to reflect the variations over time displayed by long-term movements in many economic time series.[3] A flexible, smooth, non-linear and not necessarily monotonic trend is estimated with a long-term moving average. The order of this moving average must be at least as long as the average duration of the business cycle so as to yield smooth curves that contain no significant elements of the short-term fluctuations of the series. We chose 43 as the order of the moving average, 43 being the average number of months of the cyclical fluctuations over the period 1965-1985 (OECD, 1987; Zarnowitz, 1992, p. 262).[4] This method makes it necessary to extrapolate the last 21 trend values. To this end, a specific linear extrapolation scheme is used which avoids cyclical bias of the trend estimate.

Variants on our more mechanical approach are frequently applied in comparative studies of business cycles (Danthine and Girardin, 1989, Brandner and Neusser, 1992, Smeets, 1992). A possible deficiency of this approach is that the application of moving-average or other filters may induce spurious results (Canova, 1993). An alternative methodology would be to extract the business cycle component on the basis of an elaborated model fitted individually to each time series or set of time series. Beveridge and Nelson (1981), for example, propose a decomposition based on a fitted ARIMA model for each individual series. Harvey (1985) argues in favour of a decomposition based on a so-called structural model whose characteristics differ for each series (see Clark, 1987, Ng and Young, 1990, and Harvey, 1993, for details). These alternatives are attractive from a purely statistical or econometric point of

---

[3] Stationary series such as the results of consumer and business surveys and interest rates do not, in principle, contain a trend (see Öller, 1990). If a trend is nevertheless estimated, it in fact describes temporary medium-term movements. This does not have adverse consequences for the properties of the cyclical component calculated on the basis of such trends.

[4] Alternatively, the order of the moving average could be variable and the result of a detailed analysis of individual cycles, following the methods developed by Burns and Mitchell (1946). Without denying the usefulness of the latter approach, we will be more interested in a general characterization of cyclical regularities.

view as they allow the data to determine the model parameters. On the other hand, they require some assumptions which are controversial from an economic-theoretical perspective.[5] The Beveridge-Nelson decomposition, for instance, assumes that the secular and cyclical components are perfectly correlated. On the other end, in most structural models the assumption is made that the disturbances driving the unobserved components are mutually uncorrelated (for a discussion of the consequences of this assumption, see Garcia-Ferrer and Del Hoyo, 1992a, 1992b, Young, 1992, and Harvey, 1992). This orthogonality assumption of trend and business cycle components is probably as controversial as the perfect correlation assumption of Beveridge and Nelson. Zarnowitz (1992, p. 184), for instance, argues that trend and cycles interact and cannot be clearly separated. Moreover, both the Beveridge-Nelson decomposition and the structural model approach are generally very time-consuming, which is a disadvantage if, as in our case, a very large set of variables is involved.

Canova (1993) and many others conclude that the business cycle found - and the stylized business cycle facts derived from it - depend on the method of trend estimation. Canova compares many trend estimation methods: Hodrick-Prescott (HP-4, HP-1600), Beveridge-Nelson (BN), Linear (L), First Order Differencing (FOD), Segmented (S), Unobservable Components (UC), Frequency Domain Filters (FDF) and three multivariate methods. He found that the resulting business cycles may be classified in three types of patterns. HP-1600, S, FDF and UC render more or less identical turning points corresponding with NBER dating. L and the three multivariate procedures generate long cycles with deviating turning points and the remaining methods, HP-4, FOD and BN, give short cycles and erratic results. We are interested only in the first group generating NBER-related results. One objection of Canova against using (only) one kind of detrending procedure is that the resulting business cycle is not unique. A second objection, referring to HP as well as other detrending procedures from the first group mentioned above, concerns the neglect of part of the variability of cycles longer than the average of 4 to 6 years. We do not fully agree with these objections of Canova where the present case is concerned. In preliminary analyses, we applied various methods, including HP en FOD, and came to the conclusion that the various detrending methods give more or less the same results, as Canova found for his first group of methods.[6] Moreover, the resulting business

[5] Canova (1993, p.2) concludes that neither dynamic economic theory nor the empirical literature gives an indication of the precise relationship between cyclical and secular components.

[6] Our moving-average based method yields results which are almost identical to those based on the HP-λ trend with a very high value of λ. A high value of λ seems

cycle and its turning points roughly correspond to raw yearly growth rates of GNP. Since these rates, which act as some kind of objective reference, are not biased by any detrending method, we conclude that the methods mentioned above, if applied correctly, yield fairly reliable outcomes. This meets the first objection of Canova. We also applied the Phase Average Trend (PAT) method of Boschan and Ebanks (1978), which has been used successfully in many countries (Zarnowitz, 1992). This method is capable of dealing with business cycles of varying lengths. We found that the resulting business cycles usually show only moderate deviations from, say, HP-cycles and that the turning points are comparable (Bikker and De Haan, 1990).[7] This meets the second objection of Canova. In conclusion, we find the more popular model based (detrending) procedures not always superior from a economic-theoretical point of view and too laborious for large-scale application. Empirical research indicates that mechanical procedures, like the one we use, yield satisfactory results.

Dividing the seasonally adjusted series by the corresponding trend results in a business cycle measured as a deviation from the trend. Since this may be distorted by random factors, some smoothing procedure is desirable to prevent irregular variations leading to wrong conclusions. We used a centred 12-month moving average. The order of the moving average is sufficiently low to prevent interactions with cyclical factors, which have lengths generally exceeding 30 months. The inherent loss of data is being compensated for by extrapolation based on a weighting scheme which attaches progressively more weight to the most recent data as the smoothing process reaches the end of the dataset. The smoothing procedure hardly proves to affect the main characteristics of the calculated business cycles.

4.3 Constructing a composite leading indicator

To construct a composite leading indicator, it is necessary to have a measure of a country's actual business cycle, referred to as the reference index. Using a method developed by Bry and Boschan (1971), the turning points in the cyclical pattern of this reference index are determined over the period covered. These turning points serve as the reference points against which the individual candidate leading indicators are selected. Variables are gathered which, from an economic point of view, can be expected to predict the general business climate. These variables are referred to below as basic indicators. The cyclical pattern of these basic

---

plausible as we analyse monthly data. Methods based on random walks yield results which were inferior to HP and our moving average based method.

[7] The PAT method is less suitable for predicting trends. That is the only reason for not using this method in this chapter.

indicators is compared with that of the reference index in order to determine the number of months by which the basic indicators lead the reference index, i.e. the timing. In determining the timing, we use two methods. The first places the emphasis on turning points: for each basic indicator, the average number of months by which the turning points lead those in the reference index is calculated. The second method considers not only the turning points but also the entire cyclical pattern. The measure used is the correlation between the reference index (y) and the basic indicator (x), with the latter lagging by a number of months (l) so as to maximize the correlation coefficient:

$$\rho(l) = \Sigma_t\left(y_t - \bar{y}\right)\left(x_{t+l} - \bar{x}_l\right) / \left(\Sigma_t\left(y_t - \bar{y}\right)^2 \Sigma_t\left(x_{t+l} - \bar{x}_l\right)^2\right)^{1/2} \quad (1)$$

in absolute terms. In this formula, $\bar{y}$ and $\bar{x}_l$ are the averages of y_t and x_{t+l} respectively, over t. The lead ($-l$) is the second measure. The magnitude of the correlation coefficient indicates how closely the basic indicator concerned exhibits the same cyclical pattern as the reference index. The actual timing of each basic indicator is determined by an unweighted average of the two measures. This is because a cyclical pattern which closely follows that of the reference index and the ability to predict turning points accurately are both important characteristics.

After determining the correlation between the various basic indicators and the reference index, along with the timing of the former, a selection is made according to the following criteria. Economic variables exhibiting cyclical patterns which do not reflect that of the reference index are rejected. Also, a minimum lead of 4 months is required, thus ensuring a forecast at least 4 months ahead. The third criterion is economic plausibility. The amount by which the basic indicator leads the reference index must be in line with what one would expect on the basis of economic theory (see also Auerbach, 1982). The method employed is therefore not entirely 'measurement without theory', as was suggested by Koopmans (1947). Series where the lead is implausibly large are rejected. The final criterion concerns the degree of correlation between the basic indicator and the reference index as defined in equation (1). This criterion is straightforward: a correlation of at least 0.5 is required. This boundary has been chosen as high as possible, as higher correlations correspond to better basic indicators, under the restriction that at least a sufficient number of basic indicators are selected.

The aim is to combine selected basic indicators into a single composite leading indicator to provide a clear, one-dimensional description of the general state of a country's business climate. To this end, basic indicators are normalized and synchronized. Normalization adjusts for the fact that not all the basic indicators exhibit cyclical fluctuations of the same amplitude. A transformation resulting in a zero mean and unit standard deviation is therefore applied. This prevents basic indicators with stronger fluctuations from dominating the composite indicator. The selected basic indicators are synchronised with the reference index so as to align their cyclical phases. Synchronisation thus adjusts for the different leads of the selected basic indicators. This is achieved by applying a lag to the various basic indicators equal to their respective leads. This causes the turning points of the basic indicators to coincide on average, making the cyclical pattern of the composite indicator clearer than it would be without synchronization. None of the previously cited studies carries out this process, which greatly enhances the quality of the composite indicator.

After these transformations, the selected basic indicators of one country are combined into a single composite leading indicator. Following Kloek and Bannink (1962), Burley (1971) and Fase and Bikker (1985), this was done by means of principal component analysis. Note that each transformed basic indicator consists of the business cycle component of its time series. The first principal component is the common element of the various basic indicators and is supposed to be a reflection of the business cycle.[8] With this technique, the strength of the relationship between the selected basic indicators and the business cycle (as defined by the first principal component) determines the weight given to the various basic indicators making up the composite indicator. This represents a refinement with respect to, for example, OECD (1987), in which all the basic indicators were given the same weight.

4.4 Selection of basic indicators and countries

To construct composite leading indicators, monthly data for around 50 economic variables were collected for each country.[9] In selecting variables with a predictive potential, a vitally important consideration is the economic plausibility of their leading character. Other considerations are of a practical nature, such as the availability of long time series with as few interruptions as possible and availability of the data with minimum delay. Three different kinds of variables are basically considered: variables which themselves cause changes in the level of economic activity (e.g. interest rates and raw materials prices), actual precursors of

[8] The first principal component is the best linear combination of the basic indicators, best in the sense that the particular combination of variables will account for more of the total variance of the selected basic indicators than any other linear combination of variables.

[9] For a number of countries, quarterly figures were also used, from which quasi-monthly figures were constructed with the help of the method developed by Boot et al. (1967).

activity (e.g. new orders and issue of building permits) and variables specifically relating to the future, e.g. share prices and the results of consumer and business surveys. Following Klein and Moore (1983), Fase and Bikker (1985) and Bikker and De Haan (1988), all series, with the exception of price and cost variables, are expressed in volume terms. Where only nominal data were available, the figures were deflated by the cost-of-living index or a more specific price index. As in Bikker and De Haan (1988), manufacturing output volume was used as the reference index. An alternative would be real GNP, which has the advantage of a wider coverage than the production of the manufacturing industry which, on average, in 1990 represented roughly a quarter of GNP in the countries considered. In addition, GNP is the variable given the most attention by economic forecasters. However, it is available from national sources only on a quarterly basis and the publication lag for GNP figures is considerably longer than for manufacturing output data, which are available on a monthly basis. Moreover, some expenditure components of GNP are typically non-cyclical, counter-cyclical or follow the general economic cycle with different leads and lags (OECD, 1992, Berk, 1993). Government expenditure, for example, does not follow the general economic cycle. On aggregation, these components may cause interference, which obscures the essential features of the business cycle in total GNP. So practical as well as theoretical arguments prevent the choice of GNP as reference index.

Composite leading indicators were constructed for the following countries: the United States of America (USA), Canada, Japan, Germany (excluding the former GDR), France, Italy, the United Kingdom (UK), Austria, Belgium, Denmark, Ireland, the Netherlands, Spain, Sweden and Switzerland. This list includes the world's major economies (the G-7 countries), the other countries of the EC, with the exception of Portugal and Greece,[10] two EFTA countries, and Switzerland. For the Netherlands, an indicator had previously been constructed using the method described above (Bikker and De Haan, 1988). In general, this selection of countries was also used in various comparable studies (Scholing and Timmerman, 1977; Klein and Moore, 1983). The Appendix gives a detailed summary of the basic indicators used and their sources. It is important to have information concerning the behaviour of the variables in as many business cycles as possible, which necessitates long time series. In principle, only time series starting in 1970 or earlier were included in the study. This requirement made it impossible to construct a reliable leading indicator for Greece, although a reference index - the cyclical component of

[10] Portugal was excluded because of insufficient data and Greece because the necessary time series were too short.

manufacturing output - was available, and is used in the analysis of international interdependence of business cycles.

4.5 Empirical results

Applying the method described above to the assembled data resulted in composite leading indicators for 15 countries. Table 4.1 lists the basic indicators selected for these leading indicators. For each basic indicator, the factor loading with respect to the first principal component, which is defined as the composite leading indicator, is shown. Factor loadings indicate the correlation between the basic indicators and the first principal component. This principal component can also be seen as a weighted average of the individual series. The absolute values of the factor loadings are equal to the weightings, apart from a constant.[11] Variables obtained from the business and consumer surveys are found to have the highest factor loadings and can therefore be expected to make the biggest contribution to the predictive power of the composite indicator. This probably has to do with the fact that these variables specifically relate to the future and so reflect expectations about the economy. The inverse values of the short-term interest rate and the yield curve also score high, as these variables likewise reflect expectations (Estrella and Hardouvelis, 1991; see also the second chapter of this book).

The last line of table 4.1 shows the extent to which the first principal component accounts for the variance in the basic indicators. This goodness of fit varies from 56% (Spain) to 80% (Italy) and averages 67%. Table 4.2 gives the lead of the selected basic indicators along with the average leads of the composite indicators for the various countries.The lead of the composite indicators varies from 4 to 6 months, with the exception of Austria, where the indicator has a lead of 12 months. The country leading indicators themselves are plotted together with the reference indices in figure 4.1. In these graphs, the leading indicators are lagged to facilitate comparison. For almost every country, the results show smooth and clear cyclical patterns closely coinciding with the upswings and downswings of the reference indices, the latter serving as the actual business cycle.

[11] Series which are inversely related to the business cycle have a negative factor loading. The inverse values of such series were used before weighting.

Table 4.1 Factor loadings with respect to the first principal component of the selected basic indicators (in hundredths)

	USA	Canada	Japan	Germany	France	Italy	UK	Austria	Belgium	Denmark	Ireland	Netherlands	Spain	Sweden	Switzerland	No.	Average
I Output, stocks and orders																	
Stock levels in manufacturing industry (inverse)	-54	-63	-89													3	-69
II Construction, retail sales and trade																	
Consumer spending on manufactured goods					79											1	79
New construction orders			70													1	70
Housing contracts	89															1	89
Building permits, housing		57							80							2	69
New housing orders/building permits (volume)										76						1	76
New car registrations (volume)					87		78			95			60			4	80
III Labour																	
Average working week in manufacturing (hours)	94															1	94
New unemployment benefits claims (inverse)	-93															1	-93
IV Prices, cost and profits																	
Consumer price index (inverse)	-78	-41	-93				-83			-74				-83	-74	7	-75
Long interest rate (inverse)								-90						-47		2	-69
Short interest rate (inverse)	-92	-89	-90	-84	-76	-86	-85		-91	-86	-84				-93	11	-87
Yield curve	80	82	81	69	83	75	70		80	67					89	10	78
Yield curve (inverse)								-76								1	-76
Raw materials prices, total (inverse)	-69						-69		-82		-83					4	-76
Raw materials prices, excl. energy (inverse)			-82	-67	-77			-75		-68			-74			6	-74
V Monetary and financial																	
M1	77	87	91	62	68			81	80	87	88	72	47		82	12	77
M2 (M1 + near money)			96			77								82		3	85
Share prices (volume)	83	68	53	71	58		75		80	58	92		53	68	78	12	70
New NCM policy holders (inverse)												-73				1	73
IV Consumer and business surveys																	
Level of order books						98							86	92		3	92
Order books, future tendency													89	91		2	90

Table 4.1 Factor loadings with respect to the first principal component of the selected basic indicators (in hundredths)

	USA	Canada	Japan	Germany	France	Italy	UK	Austria	Belgium	Denmark	Ireland	Netherlands	Spain	Sweden	Switzerland	No.	Average
Change in stocks of finished products (inverse)		-89				-98										2	-94
Future movements in output		93			93		84			86				95	87	6	90
Production expectations				85	95	94	82					91	95			6	90
Index of consumer confidence				88	78		84		79	86						5	83
Order inflow, future tendency		91				94										2	93
Actual order inflow												93				1	93
Construction industry confidence indicator				93												1	93
Construction industry order books				86												1	86
Employment expectations				93												1	93
Expectations of selling prices									83							1	83
Stocks of finished products (inverse)						-97							-79	-92		3	-89
General economic outlook					85	82	78									3	82
IFO business climate indicator Germany												88				1	88
Number of basic indicators per country	10	10	9	10	11	9	10	4	8	10	4	5	8	8	6		
Goodness of fit[1]	67	61	70	65	65	80	63	65	68	63	75	71	56	68	65		67

[1] Percentage of the movement in the basic indicators accounted for by the first principal component

Table 4.2 Leads (-) of selected basic components relative to reference indices [1]) (in months)

	USA	Canada	Japan	Germany	France	Italy	UK	Austria	Belgium	Denmark	Ireland	Netherlands	Spain	Sweden	Switzerland	No.	Average
I Output, stocks and orders																	
Stock levels in manufacturing industry (inverse)	-7	-7	-5													3	-6
II Construction, retail sales and trade																	
Consumer spending on manufactured goods					-4											1	-4
New construction orders			-4													1	-4
Housing contracts	-7															1	-7
Building permits, housing		-6							-4							2	-5
New housing orders/building permits (volume)										-5						1	-5
New car registrations (volume)					-4		-8			-5			-4			4	-5
III Labour																	
Average working week in manufacturing (hours)	-4															1	-4
New unemployment benefits claims (inverse)	-4															1	-4
IV Prices, cost and profits																	
Consumer price index (inverse)	-8	-6	-9				-6			-5				-7	-6	7	-7
Long interest rate (inverse)								-13						-17		2	-15
Short interest rate (inverse)	-17	-15	-12	-17	-14	-13	-16		-15	-8	-14				-20	11	-14
Yield curve	-16	-15	-10	-18	-15	-18	-20		-7	-9					-21	10	-15
Yield curve (inverse)								-12								1	-12
Raw materials prices, total (inverse)	-11						-13		-16		-11					4	-13
Raw materials prices, excl. energy (inverse)			-14	-15	-14			-17		-11			-19			6	-15
V Monetary and financial																	
M1	-7	-6	-5	-11	-8			-13	-9	-5	-4	-17	-8		-14	12	-9
M2 (M1 + near money)			-7			-9								-10		3	-9
Share prices (volume)	-8	-5	-8	-9	-5		-10		-16	-4	-6		-4	-9	-7	12	-8
New NCM policy holders (inverse)												-7				1	-7
IV Consumer and business surveys																	
Level of order books						-8							-4	-5		3	-6
Order books, future tendency													-10	-10		2	-10
Change in stocks of finished products (inverse)		-4				-6										2	-5
Future movements in output		-5			-5		-5			-6				-9	-6	6	-6
Production expectations				-7	-4	-4	-6					-5	-7			6	-6
Index of consumer confidence				-10	-8		-11		-4	-8						5	-8

Table 4.2 Leads (-) of selected basic components relative to reference indices [1]) (in months)

	USA	Canada	Japan	Germany	France	Italy	UK	Austria	Belgium	Denmark	Ireland	Netherlands	Spain	Sweden	Switzerland	No.	Average
Order inflow, future tendency		-5				-8										2	-6
Actual order inflow												-7				1	-7
Construction industry confidence indicator				-8												1	-8
Construction industry order books				-6												1	-6
Employment expectations				-9												1	-9
Expectations of selling prices									-4							1	-4
Stocks of finished products (inverse)						-4							-5	-6		3	-5
General economic outlook					-4	-8	-10									3	-7
IFO business climate indicator Germany												-6				1	-6
Number of basic indicators per country	10	10	9	10	11	9	10	4	8	10	4	5	8	8	6		
Average lead of the composite indicator	-4	-4	-4	-6	-4	-4	-5	-12	-4	-4	-4	-5	-4	-5	-6		

[1] Series marked 'inverse' display a cyclical pattern with a negative correlation to that of the reference indices

Figure 4.1 Composite leading indicators for various countries

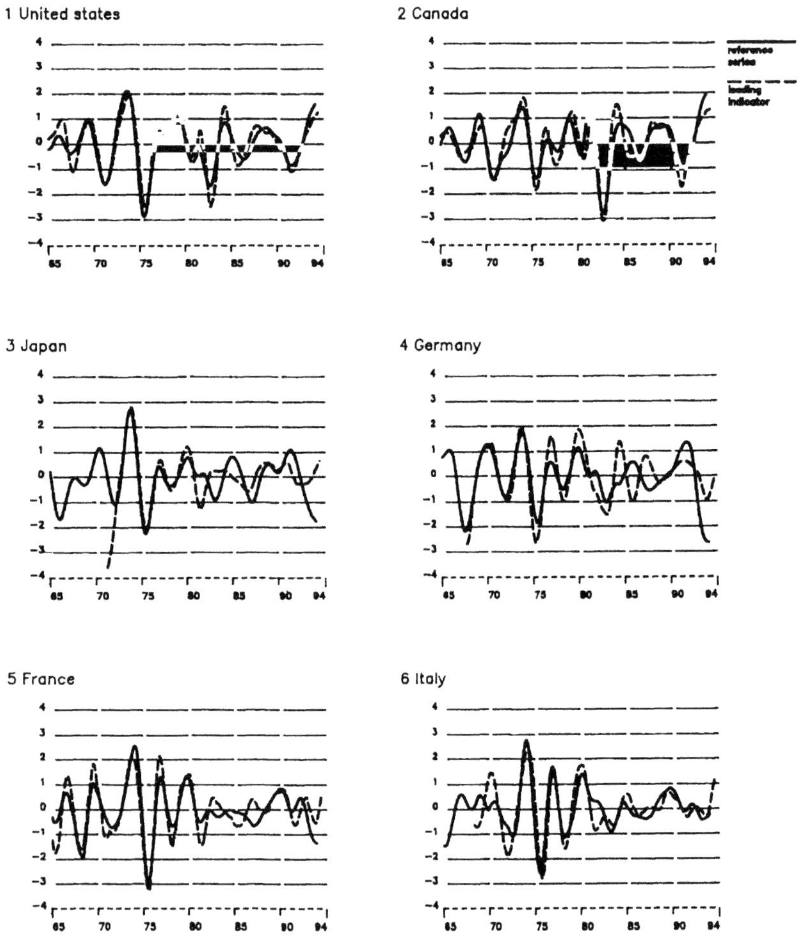

Figure 4.1 Composite leading indicators for various countries

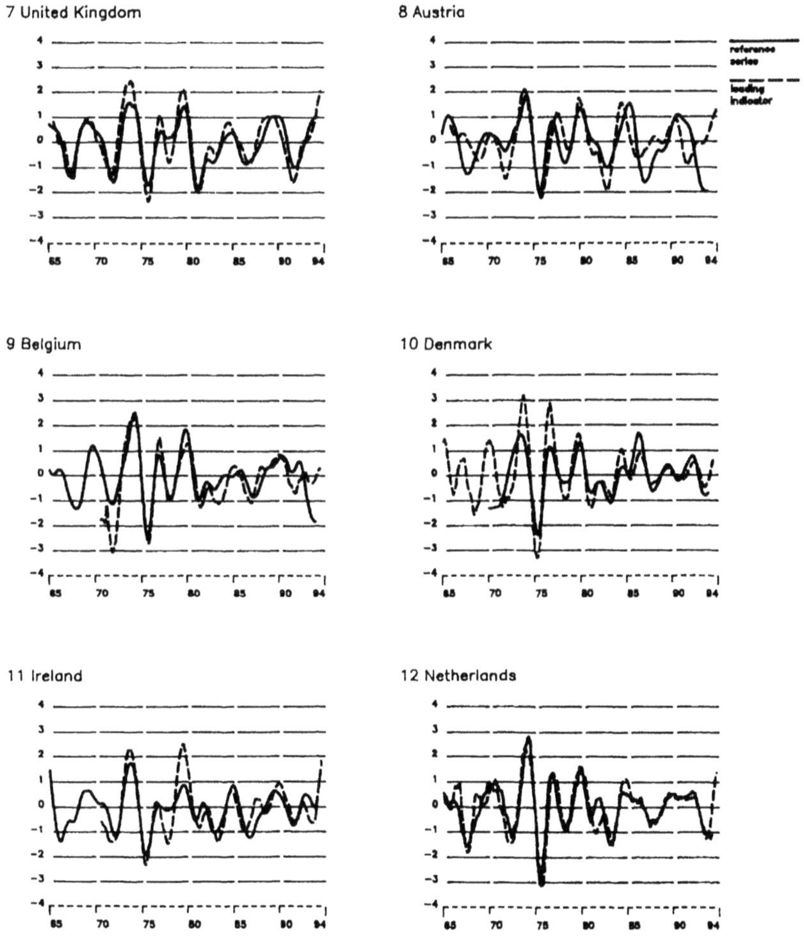

Figure 4.1 Composite leading indicators for various countries

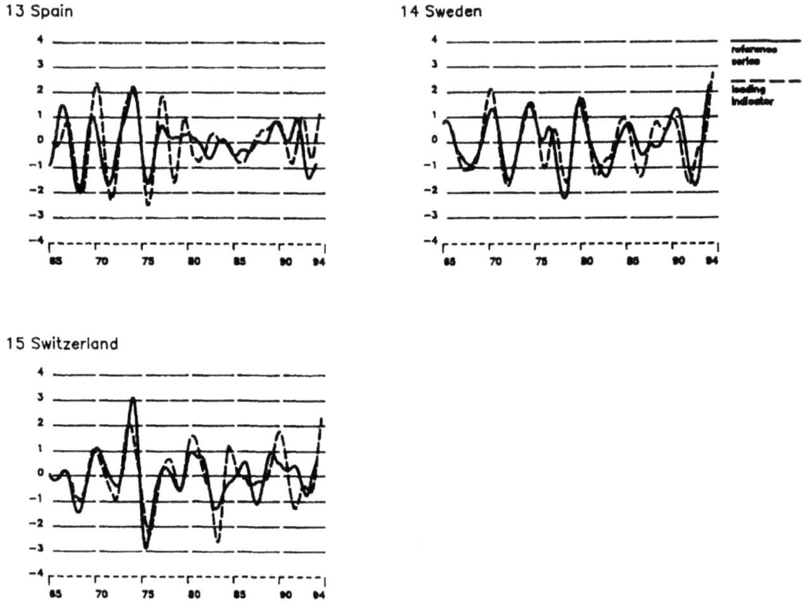

Table 4.3 shows the correlations between the composite indicators and the reference indices, providing a measure of the quality of the national leading indicators. It may be concluded that the method used generates composite leading indicators which, over the period covered, are fairly close approximations of the movements in the reference indices for most of the countries. Surprisingly, especially in view of the high correlations for the other major countries such as the USA, Japan, and the UK, there is a relatively low correlation between the leading indicator and the reference index for Germany. This low correlation is also apparent from graph 4 in figure 4.1 and is probably due to a different cyclical development of manufacturing output (the reference index) in the middle of the 1980s which is attributable to the major strike in the German engineering industry in 1984.[12] The negative effect this had on production was as large as the average economic slowdown in periods of recession. This effect of the strike obviously could not be predicted and is therefore not reflected in any of the selected basic indicators.

Table 4.3: Correlation between composite indicators and reference indices

USA (US)	0.93
Canada (CA)	0.90
Japan (JP)	0.86
Germany (DE)	0.74
France (FR)	0.89
Italy (IT)	0.87
UK (GB)	0.90
Austria (AT)	0.70
Belgium (BE)	0.91
Denmark (DK)	0.87
Ireland (IE)	0.83
Netherlands (NL)	0.91
Spain (ES)	0.79
Sweden (SE)	0.81
Switzerland (CH)	0.73

Explanatory note: The ISO country codes between parentheses are used in Table 5.

The correlations of table 4.3 refer to the *ex post* forecasting quality. The *ex ante* forecasting performance has been investigated for the Dutch leading indicator, which has been published monthly since December 1988 (Bikker and De Haan, 1988). It was concluded that all actual turning points were forecasted and no turning points were predicted which did not actually occur later. The mean absolute difference between 35 monthly predictions and realizations in 1988-91 has been 0.18 (Fase, 1992), which

[12] The German leading indicators constructed by the OECD and the IFO also perform relatively poorly, especially in the mid-80s.

is, strikingly enough, lower than in the sample period (0.33).

Berk and Bikker (1994) present root mean squared errors (RMSE) of industrial production growth and GDP growth based on these indicators. On the whole, the RMSE of the indicators are more or less equal to those of the elaborate macro-economic models. For instance, our RMSE of GDP growth in the Netherlands is 0.78%, which compares favourably with the RMSE of Dutch macro-economic structural models (1.06% and higher; CPB, 1992).

4.6 International interdependence of business cycles

The reference indices developed above for a number of countries including the world's major economies can be used to perform a closer analysis of international economic interdependence. The influence of the business cycle in one country on that of another is directed partly along quantifiable channels such as trade flows and interest rates, which have sizeable impacts on spending. Besides these, however, there are many channels through which business cycle impulses can be transmitted which are not directly measurable: investment decisions, spending decisions and many other kinds of decisions are based on expectations regarding the future business climate, in which foreign factors play a part. These expectations, which are mainly identified through business and consumer surveys, play an important part in the international interdependence of cyclical movements in the economy. Using the calculated reference indices, their ultimate direct and indirect effects can be observed and analysed.

There have been numerous developments contributing to closer international co-operation, such as the removal of trade barriers, deregulation of capital markets, greatly improved communications and the international expansion of businesses. The increasing economic integration within the EC over the years plays a particularly important part in this. Integration prior to 1970, the start of the period covered by this study, probably caused the six original EEC countries already to be more closely linked than average in 1970. Part of this interdependence of the EEC countries must be attributed to their geographical location (see, for example, Bikker, 1987). Since 1970, we might reasonably expect to see a closer interdependence within the EC as the Community expanded. It is also likely that international interdependence has become stronger over the years by virtue of worldwide economic integration. Below we investigate these suppositions regarding the international interdependence of business cycles in greater detail.

For this purpose, principal component analysis was applied to the reference indices of the 16 countries in the study (including Greece).

Following the methodology used in the construction of the national composite leading indicators, we interpret the first principal component as the international business cycle (Scholing and Timmerman, 1977; Fuhrmann, 1980). It must be borne in mind, however, that this takes no account of the size of individual countries. The first principal component accounts for as much as possible of the variance in the reference indices of the various countries, 67% of the total variance in fact being explained by this component (last row in table 4.4). The factor loadings pertaining to the first principal component give an indication of the correlation between the business cycle in the countries concerned and the international business cycle. Over the period 1971-1990, Japan and the European countries of France, Belgium, Germany and the Netherlands, with correlations in excess of 90%, proved to be the most internationally orientated (see table 4.4; cf. also Bikker, 1993). Then comes Ireland, Italy, the USA, Switzerland and Austria, with correlations in excess of 80%, and Spain and the UK, Denmark, Greece and Canada with correlations in excess of 70%. With a correlation of 57%, the Swedish economy was found to have the weakest link with other countries. This result is very much in line with expectations: the EC countries score high, partly because of their geographical position, with the original members of the EC scoring higher than the newer member states. Japan's economy is closely linked to those of other countries. It appears that the Japanese economy is more export-led than determined by domestic policy, for example. Several European countries exhibit a business cycle pattern which is less affected by events abroad, either because they pursue more of an independent policy (UK), or because they are less orientated towards the other countries in the study (Greece and Sweden). Taking the present countries of the EC or of the EEA (EC plus EFTA) together, we find that the factor loadings do not differ by a great deal: the old EEC countries plus Ireland score highest. The first principal component of the EFTA countries is found to correlate equally with the three individual countries concerned. In other words, Sweden is found not to be exceptional. The three overseas countries (OC) clearly divide into two blocks: North America and Japan. It is, of course, hardly surprising that the Canadian business cycle should closely match that of the USA. But it is rather surprising to find that the link between Japan and the USA is far less pronounced than between Japan and Europe.

Dividing the period into four subperiods reveals a clear shift in the international interdependence of business cycles. In contrast to what the tendency towards further internationalisation might lead one to expect, the degree of interdependence, measured in terms of the average factor loadings and the goodness of fit, is found to have become less rather than more. The first five-year period shows the closest correlation.

Table 4.4 **Factor loadings for the first principal component of the reference indices of 16 countries (in hundredths)**

	1971-90					World				EC			
	World	EC	EFTA	OC	EEA	1971-5	1976-80	1981-5	1986-90	1971-5	1976-80	1981-8	1986-90
USA	83			95		94	29	88	85				
Canada	70			91		96	32	85	86				
Japan	93			67		96	92	97	78				
Germany	90	89			90	98	96	87	4	98	93	81	-4
France	93	96			94	98	97	26	97	98	97	56	99
Italy	85	86			87	93	79	68	85	92	73	57	93
UK	77	79			77	90	67	38	89	90	72	56	92
Belgium	91	94			94	97	99	47	83	96	99	68	74
Denmark	76	77			75	81	81	84	29	82	85	90	39
Greece	71	72			69	73	62	54	78	75	66	55	82
Ireland	89	86			86	94	66	86	88	95	72	74	82
Netherlands	90	89			91	92	97	98	39	92	97	93	32
Spain	79	80			78	94	34	-28	69	92	31	-48	78
Austria	81		83		82	92	87	89	53				
Sweden	57		82		59	49	84	86	88				
Switzerland	82		87		82	96	26	76	69				
Goodness of fit [1]	67	72	71	73	68	82	56	56	55	84	66	48	54

[1] Percentage of the movement in the reference indices accounted for by the first principal component

Note 'EFTA' includes Austria and Sweden as well as Switzerland.

This period includes the first oil crisis, however, which affected all the countries simultaneously with the same intensity.[13] The international interdependence suggested by this does not point to economic integration but to common dependence on an external factor. It is therefore not really possible to compare the correlation for this period with that found in the later five-year periods in which no such extreme shocks occurred. The later periods all show similar results. This is surprising, however, since the period 1976-1980 was one of more pronounced cyclical movements than the subsequent five-year periods, as shown by figure 4.1. This is reflected by occasionally very small and even negative factor loadings in the years 1981-1990, as in the case of Germany and Spain, for example. Similar calculations by Ginsburg (1973) for the period 1955-1970 also did not indicate growing international economic interdependence. Scholing and Timmerman (1977), however, did find evidence of growing integration for the period 1961-1975. Also, as in the above analysis, the 'apparent' correlation in the five-year period 1971-1975 was found to be considerably greater than in the previous five-year periods.

The conclusion is that economic interdependence between the different countries is particularly strong in Europe and that the Japanese business cycle is closely linked to the state of the economy in Europe, the link with North America being less pronounced. Analysis according to subperiods does not reveal any tendency towards greater integration over time. Although the five-year period 1971-1975 shows evidence of strong interdependence, this can be attributed to the effect of the first oil crisis.

4.7 National indicators with an international component

The high degree of international interdependence of business cycles implies that economic activity in countries with leading cycles contains information regarding the future level of activity in the lagging economies. From this we might expect the incorporation of leading indicators for leading economies in the national composite indicators of other countries to improve the latter's predictive quality. In selecting countries whose leading indicators are included as components in the various national composite indicators, use was made of correlation analysis. Each pair of countries whose business cycles (i.e. reference indices) are highly correlated basically produces a candidate. The lead of the candidate country's leading indicator over the leading indicator for the lagging economy was obtained by maximising the correlation from equation (1) in

[13] The question of whether the cyclical movements induced by the oil crisis contain some structural elements in the sense that this crisis also produced a structural break in the trend is beyond the scope of this chapter.

terms of l.

The American economy has a worldwide function as an engine of growth, so that there is no point in adding the indicators of other countries to the indicator of the USA. Greece is not considered here because of the absence of a leading indicator and Denmark and Ireland have been ignored because the correlation analysis showed inexplicable leads of their business cycles with respect to the other countries. That leaves us with twelve other countries whose national leading indicators can usefully be expanded to include leading indicators of other countries. In addition to the indicators for leading economies, indicators for coincident economies have also been used as components in the case of a number of countries. The argument here is that even indicators of this nature might contain additional information augmenting the domestic basic indicators. In assessing the *ex post* predictive power of the improved composite leading indicators, the correlation for each country between leading indicator and reference index was again used, as above.

Table 4.5: Correlation between leading indicators and reference indices

	Incorporating other countries' indicators		Leading indicators of other countries added
	No	Yes	
Japan	0.86	0.87	US
Germany	0.74	0.78	US,JP
France	0.89	0.92	US,JP,DE,BE,IT
Italy	0.87	0.88	DE,BE,FR,ES
United Kingdom	0.90	0.91	US
Austria	0.91	0.92	JP,DE,FR,IT
Belgium	0.79	0.85	US,JP,DE
Spain	0.70	0.79	DE,NL,BE
Switzerland	0.73	0.77	US,JP,DE

Table 4.5 shows that, for nine out of the twelve countries, the correlation between the composite leading indicator and the reference indices increases when the national leading indicator has been expanded with leading indicators from one or more other countries. The first exception is the Netherlands, where there is no difference between the 'old' and 'new' leading indicators. The old Dutch indicator, however, is the only one which already included a foreign component, i.e. the IFO business climate indicator for German manufacturing industry (see table 4.1). This indicator is apparently a sufficiently good barometer of activity abroad as far as the Netherlands is concerned. For Sweden, too, the inclusion of foreign indicators as components do not improve the national indicator, thereby confirming the result attained in the previous section. For the Canadian indicator, only the indicator for the USA is a candidate as an

additional component. Adding this indicator does not provide a stronger correlation, however. For the other nine countries, it was found that including the indicators of the well-known leading economies - the USA, Japan and Germany - and, especially in continental Europe, the indicators of neighbouring economies improves the predictive power of the national composite indicators.

4.8 Conclusion

International leading economic indicators are important and popular tools in analysing and forecasting the state of the business cycle. The leading indicators constructed by the OECD, for example, are widely used by practitioners of macroeconomic forecasting. The composite leading indicators presented in this chapter are comparable to the latter indicators, but are based on an improved method, which enhances their quality. The indicators give a clear picture of the turning points and intensity of the movements in the business cycles in manufacturing industry in fifteen countries. These indicators exhibit a fairly high correlation with the actual business cycle as represented by the reference indices, while running between 4 and 6 months ahead. Monthly published predictions of the Dutch leading indicator showed a satisfactory degree of *ex ante* out-of-sample forecast performance. Our analysis shows that by using the interdependence of the business cycles the forecasting power of the national composite leading indicators can be enhanced further.

The method used to calculate the business cycle - by eliminating trend, season and random factors - makes our results dependent on the signal processing methodology used. Our approach, based on i.e. moving average filters, yields reliable outcomes while being suitable for large-scale application, which was important considering the large number of time series to be analysed. Notwithstanding, the abovementioned dependency makes it an interesting topic for future research to investigate the possible value of recently developed methods of signal processing, such as structural time-series models, in constructing leading indicators for a large number of countries.

Table A1. Source of reference indices and basis indicators: selected basic indicators are in bold type

	USA	Canada	Japan	Germany	France	Italy	UK	Austria	Belgium	Denmark	Ireland	Netherlands	Spain	Sweden	Switzerland
I Output, stocks and orders															
Manufacturing output (reference indices)	a	a	a	a	a	a	a	a	a	b	a	e	a	a	a
Net new manufacturing orders, domestic (value)								a							
Net new manufacturing orders, export (value)								a							
Net new manufacturing orders, total (value)	a	a								a					
Net new manufacturing orders, total (volume)				a										a	a
New manufacturing orders, total						a									
Net new engineering orders, total (volume)							a								
Net new equipment orders, excl. ships (value)			a												
Net new metal product orders									a						
Manufacturing industry order books, durable goods (value)	a														
Manufacturers' stock levels, total (value)	**a**	a													
Manufacturers' stock levels, total (volume)			**a**												
Manufacturers' stock levels, semimanufactures (volume)			a												
Manufacturers' stock levels, finished products		**a**													
Change in manufacturers' stock levels, total							a								
Change in manufacturers' stock levels, finished products							a								
Change in manufacturers' stock levels, semi manfacturers														a	
Manufacturing stocks versus deliveries			a												
Stock levels in the economy as a whole, change								a							
II Construction, retail sales and trade															
Retail sales, (volume)		a		a	a				a	a	a	e	a	a	
Retail sales, (value)	a					a	a	a				e			
Consumer spending on manufactured goods					**a**										
New contruction orders (value)			**a**												
New housing construction orders (value)			a												

Table A1. Continued

	USA	Canada	Japan	Germany	France	Italy	UK	Austria	Belgium	Denmark	Ireland	Netherlands	Spain	Sweden	Switzerland
New contruction orders (volume)							a								
New housing contruction orders (volume)							a								
Current housing projects														a	
Total construction contracts (value)	a														
Housing construction contracts (value)	a														
Building permits, total (value)		a		a								e			
Building permits,housing (value)		a		a								e			
Building permits, total excl. housing (value)		a													
Building permits, total (volume)									a						
Building permits, housing (volume)					a				a				a		a
New housing orders/building permits, (volume)										a					
Housing completion (value)				a											
General & Industrial building completion (value)				a											
Housing starts	a									a		e			a
Contract starts, total									a	a					
New car registration					a	a	a	a	a	a	a		a	a	a
III Labour															
Job vacancies			a	a	a		a	a	a	a		e		a	a
Job advertisements	a	a													
Average working week in manufacturing (hours)	a					a	a		a						
New unemployment benefits claims	a				a										
IV Prices, cost and profits															
Construction costs, housing				a	a	a		a		a					
Construction costs, overall	a										a				a
Cost of living index	a	a	a	a	a	a	a	a	a	a	d		a	a	a
Producer price index	a												a	a	
Long interest rate	b	a	b	b	b	b	b	a	b	b	a	e		a	a
Short interest rate	b	a	b	b	b	b	b	a	b	b	a				a
Yield curve	b	a	b	b	b	b	b	a	b	b	a				a
Raw materials prices, total	d	d	d	d	d	d	d	d	d	d	a	d	d	d	d
Raw materials prices, excl. energy	d	d	d	d	d	d	d	d	d	d	d	d	d	d	d

Table A1. Continued

	USA	Canada	Japan	Germany	France	Italy	UK	Austria	Belgium	Denmark	Ireland	Netherlands	Spain	Sweden	Switzerland
V Monetary/financial															
M1	a	a	a	a	a	a		a	a	a		g	a		a
M2 (M1 + near-money)	a	a	a	a	a	a	a	a	a	a		g	a	a	a
M3	a											e			
Share prices (value)	a	a	a	a	a	a	a	a	a	a	a	e	a	a	a
Share prices (volume)	a	a	a	a	a	a	a		a	a	a		a	a	a
Lending, domestic					a			a						a	
Lending by commercial banks	a	a								a				a	
Lending to private sector and institutions												g	a		
Lending, short term				a											a
Lending, medium and long-term				a											
Lending to industry							a								
Lending and investment incl. government bonds	a														
Net new capital issues by companies	a	a			a									a	a
Net new bond issues						a				a					
Net new bond issues by companies			a												
Savings balances with commercial banks		a													
Savings balances												g			a
Domestic bank balances							a								
Personel savings deposits				a											
Consumer credit debt	a	a													
Lending by monetary institutions									a						
Lending by non-monetary institustions									a						
New NCM policy holders												f			
VI Economic surveys															
Level of order books					c	a		a				e	a	a	a
Change in level of unfilled orders		a													
Order position				c	c	a			c		c				a
Export orders					c	c			c						
Order books, future tendency													a	a	

Table A1. Continued

	USA	Canada	Japan	Germany	France	Italy	UK	Austria	Belgium	Denmark	Ireland	Netherlands	Spain	Sweden	Switzerland
Change in stocks of finished products		a	a	c	c	a		a	c		c				a
Future changes in output		a			c		a			a				a	a
Production expectations				c	a	c	a		c		c	e	a		
Index of consumer confidence				c	c	c	a		c	c	c				
Order inflow, future tendency		a			c	c									
Actual order inflow												e			
Manufacturing industry confidence indicator				c	c	c			c		c				
Construction industry confidence indicator				c	c	c			c						
Contruction industry order books				c					c						
Employment expectations				c	c	c			c		c				
Expectations of selling prices				c	c	c			c	c					
Production capacity, future tendency			a												
Change in general situation							a								
Change in current economic situation			a												
Change in future economic situation			a												
Stocks of finished product					a	c							a	a	
Prospects for manufacturing					a										
General economic outlook						a									
IFO business climate indicator Germany												a			

Sources: a= OECD Main Economic Indicators; b= BIS-databank; c= EC-databank; d=HWWA Institut für Wirtschaftsforschung, Hamburg; e=Dutch Central Bureau of Statistics; f=NCM; g=De Nederlandsche Bank (Dutch Central Bank).

5 MEASURING INFLATION EXPECTATIONS: A SURVEY DATA APPROACH[1]

5.1 Introduction

Expectations of inflation can be important determinants of actual inflation because they influence the process of wage bargaining, price setting, speculative buying and financial investing decisions (Englander and Stone, 1989). A central bank, given its primary objective of price stability, therefore takes a natural interest in inflationary expectations of economic agents. In fact, as illustrated by the theoretical work of, e.g., Kydland and Prescott (1977) and Barro and Gordon (1983), inflationary expectations of the public are an important factor determining the success of the central bank in achieving its policy goal. Measures of inflation expectations can be used for monetary policy purposes, for example as information variables in the sense defined by Friedman (1993), or as intermediate targets in the so-called direct inflation targeting strategy (Svensson, 1996; Fuhrer, 1997).

There are in principle two methods of obtaining measures of inflation expectations. In the first method an economic model is chosen that includes expectations as variables and certain assumptions about how these expectations are formed. Estimating and solving the model then generates projected values for, e.g., the inflation rate. In this case, empirical analysis of the expectations can be carried out only indirectly, and is conditional on the behavioural model. This means that conclusions concerning the expectations will not be invariant to the choice of the underlying behavioural model (Kuismanen and Spolander, 1994). With the development of structural macroeconomic models and the rational expectations hypothesis (Muth, 1961), this line of inquiry became increasingly popular.

An alternative to this modelling of price expectations is to introduce some direct measure of price expectations. These measures have been based on either sample surveys or financial market indicators. In this chapter we will develop direct measures of inflation expectations based on consumer surveys in the Netherlands. The contribution of the chapter is twofold. First, the method we use for extracting measures of expected inflation is an extension of the well-known Carlson-Parkin (1977)

[1] Reprinted from Applied Economics, 31 (1999), J.M. Berk, "Measuring Inflation Expectations: A Survey Data Approach", 1467-1480, © 1999 with kind permission from Routledge Journals.

approach.[2] Compared to the latter, however, our method requires less restrictive assumptions. Second, in our empirical analysis we explicitly investigate the effects of deviations from the standard assumption of normally distributed price expectations, i.e. peakedness and asymmetry. Moreover, our analysis of the information content of measures of expected inflation is relevant for monetary policy purposes, in particular in the context of the recently developed direct inflation targeting approach (Green, 1996; Bernanke and Mishkin, 1997).

This chapter is organised as follows. The second section discusses the econometric issues involved in calculating inflation expectations from survey data. Section three applies these methods to Dutch data, and results in various time series of inflation expectations. Section four discusses the information content of these expectations. Section five concludes.

5.2 On the estimation of inflationary expectations from qualitative responses

The selection process of the method we use for extracting measures of expected inflation is influenced by the particular form in which the survey data are presented. The Dutch consumer survey is comparable to (in fact is a part of) the surveys conducted monthly by the European Commission. The latter ones, which are analysed by Simmons and Weiserbs (1992), Madsen (1996) and Papadia (1983), are polychotomous tendency surveys (Pesaran, 1987). In this type of survey respondents are questioned only about the expected direction of change, and can choose between more than three (but a finite number) of categories when responding. More specifically, Dutch consumers are asked the following questions regarding prices:

1. Is the price level now compared to 12 months ago a) much higher, b) moderately higher, c) a little higher, d) the same, e) lower?

2. Do you expect prices over the next 12 months a) to rise faster, b) to show a similar rise, c) to rise less fast, d) to stay the same, e) to decline?[3]

---

[2] The Carlson-Parkin or CP-method was first employed by Theil (1952) in order to provide an alternative theoretical justification for Andersons' (1951, 1952) use of balance statistics to quantify the results obtained from the monthly surveys held by the IFO Institute in Munich. Balance statistics are defined as the difference between the percentage of respondents who report an increase of, say, prices, and the percentage of respondents reporting a decrease.

[3] Both questions also include a 'don't know' category. In what follows, we allocate the numbers of this category proportionally to the other response categories. See Visco (1984, pp. 30,32) for a discussion.

Our variant of the CP method is applicable to polychotomous tendency surveys in which respondents are asked questions about currently perceived inflation rates as well as expected future inflation rates. The quantification of qualitative expectations is achieved by exploiting the fact that the question regarding future price movements 'links' the answer about the expected rate of inflation to the rate currently perceived and that two of the options which are open to the respondent are quantitative in nature (i.e. the 'no change in inflation' and 'no change in prices' options).

An informal description of our method runs as follows (for a formal derivation, see the Appendix). Within a cross-sectional sample of size N surveyed at time t, each agent i is supposed to answer questions about the future behaviour of prices at time $t+12$ (in months) on the basis of a subjective conditional probability distribution. This distribution is conditional on the information set available to the consumer at t. Agents are then supposed to report that no change in the price level is expected if the expected future inflation rate falls within an interval centered around zero. Similarly, agents will report that no change in the rate of inflation is expected if their expectation falls within an interval centered on the price increase that they perceived to have occurred in the past 12 months. The boundaries of both intervals, denoted as the response thresholds, are to be determined by the data. Given the assumptions outlined in the Appendix, the survey results can be regarded as N drawings from the aggregate population. We are in particular interested in the centrality measure of this distribution, representing the average inflation rate expected by consumers in the survey.[4] Additional assumptions enable us to derive expressions of this expected inflation rate, the standard deviation and the response thresholds as functions of the survey responses. These expressions are given in relation to the perceived inflation rate, i.e. the price rise that consumers perceive to have occurred in the past 12 months. In order to obtain actual values for these variables, it is necessary to make two additional assumptions. First, the form of the aggregate density function must be known completely (except for its first and second moments). Second, the perceived inflation rate over the last 12 months must be known. We will discuss each of these additional assumptions in turn.

5.2.1 The distribution of inflation expectations

In most empirical applications of the CP-method the normal distribution is

[4] For monetary policy, the dispersion measure of this distribution is also of interest, since it proxies the inflation uncertainty expected by consumers (Juster and Taylor, 1975; Chan-Lee, 1980). Our method also generates estimates of this dispersion measure, but space limitations force us in this paper to concentrate on the information content of the centrality measure.

used (Seitz, 1988).[5] Our assumptions will ensure that the aggregate distribution of price changes expected by consumers in the survey is in fact the sum of independent identically distributed random variables (generated by the subjective distributions, each having finite first and second moments). Then the Central Limit Theorem (Kendall and Stuart, 1977) applies, and the aggregate distribution is normal. The normality assumption is also convenient: its statistical theory has been extensively developed, it is completely specified by two parameters and it is extensively tabulated, which makes the necessary computations easier to handle. However, the normal distribution also has certain disadvantages. As noted by, *inter alia*, Batchelor (1981, 1982), Visco (1984) and Foster and Gregory (1977), there are *a priori* reasons for assuming that the aggregate distribution of expectations is not symmetric.[6] More specifically, with an upward trend in prices, the distribution of answers might be skewed to the right (Theil, 1952). In fact, Carlson (1975) and Vining and Elwertowski (1976), studying the distribution of individual inflation expectations and the distribution of individual inflation rates in the US, find two non-normal features: the survey responses are more centrally peaked and tend to be distributed asymmetrically (more specifically, there is positive (negative) skewness during high (low) inflationary periods). Imposing a normal distribution then yields downward (upward) biased estimates of the expected inflation rate during high (low) inflationary periods (Smith and McAleer, 1990). The results of Pesaran (1987) and Pesaran and Wright (1991) seem to confirm this. Normality was also rejected by Batchelor (1981) and Batchelor and Dua (1987) for French, German and UK data. However, Balcombe (1996), using consumer survey data from New Zealand, extends the CP approach to allow for skewness and kurtotic distributions but finds no empirical evidence in favour of such distributions. Conclusive empirical evidence concerning the form of the distribution is difficult to obtain, as it requires surveys for which the microresponses are not only available (which is often not the case for privacy reasons), but also quantitative in form. In light of the previous discussion, and without access to data on quantitative price changes of individual consumers, which would allow us to check the accuracy of alternative distributional assumptions, different types of distributions will be used and tested for their appropriateness. We start by following existing practice and use the normal distribution. In addition, we use a scaled-*t* distribution. There are several reasons for choosing this type of distribution. First, the *t*-distribution can be motivated in exactly the same way as the

[5] For details regarding this and the other distributions used in this paper, see Johnson and Kotz (1970).

[6] Also, the maximum negative outcome is by definition limited, whereas the maximum positive response is, in theory, unbounded. This also suggests skewness to the right.

normal distribution. This is because our appeal to the Central Limit Theorem above was unnecessarily restrictive (Batchelor, 1981). In general this Theorem states that the sum of independent, identically distributed, random variables will tend to some particular class of distributions (the family of 'stable laws'), of which the normal distribution is but one example and of which the *t*-distribution is also a member. Second, research by Carlson (1975) has shown that a symmetrically scaled *t*-distribution provides a better approximation to the distribution of inflationary expectations than the normal distribution, in particular because of its peakedness.[7] Third, it can be modified relatively easily to incorporate asymmetry, and a comparison of central-*t* and noncentral-*t* gives an indication of the effects of asymmetry on measures of inflation expectations. In sum, by using normal, central-*t* and noncentral-*t* distributions we allow for nonnormal peakedness as well as asymmetry to influence our expectation measures.

For the qualitative surveys which we are considering, however, there are not enough independent response categories to estimate other distributional parameters besides the mean and standard deviation. The degrees of freedom and the asymmetry-parameter therefore have to be determined outside the model. Regarding the degrees of freedom, we use (for the central-*t* as well as the noncentral-*t* distribution) the result of Carlson (1975) who finds that a number equal to six gives the best estimates. With respect to the asymmetry parameter relevant for the noncentral-*t*, we assume that the degree of asymmetry varies directly with the level of inflation: as the inflation rate increases (decreases), the proportion of consumers expecting an increase in future prices will increase (decrease) as well. We use two measures of asymmetry, both of them time-varying. In the first measure, the degree of asymmetry is measured as the difference between the last official inflation rate available to consumers when responding to the survey, and the average of (twelve month) inflation rates in the previous 12 months.[8] The second measure follows Batchelor (1981), and uses the deviation of actual inflation during each month from its mean over the whole sample period.

[7] The preference of Carlson (1975) for the scaled *t*-distribution was based on empirical, not theoretical, grounds. In turned out that this distribution provided the best fit to the observed subjective distributions of respondents to the Livingston survey in the US.

[8] i.e. $asym(t) = \Pi(t-1) - \sum_{i=1}^{12} \Pi(t-i-1)/12$, thereby assuming that consumers have a horizon of 12 months when using past information, and that the inflation outcome in each of these months has an equal influence on the consumers' expectations.

5.2.2 The perceived inflation rate

As shown in the Appendix, the perceived past inflation rate performs a scaling role with respect to the expected future inflation rate. A possible proxy for this perceived rate is the most recent inflation rate available to consumers when answering the survey question regarding future prices (Simmons and Weiserbs, 1992). More specifically, given the publication lag involved this would imply: $\Pi_t^p = \Pi_{t-1} = \ln(cpi_{t-1}) - \ln(cpi_{t-13})$. However, there is no *a priori* reason to expect that the inflation rate perceived by consumers is adequately and completely represented by official inflation figures. In fact, due to the 'signal processing problem' described in Lucas (1972, 1976), respondents to the survey, even if behaving rationally, may not perceive correctly the aggregate inflation rate. An alternative measure of the perceived inflation rate makes use of survey information, i.e. the answers of consumers to the question pertaining to price developments in the past 12 months. But we have to take into account the fact that the two questions regarding prices in the survey are phrased differently. We therefore transformed the first question by aggregating the responses pertaining to different intensities of inflation (i.e. prices in the past 12 months are 'much higher', 'moderately higher' and 'weakly higher') into 'positive inflation' (R_t). Together with the categories 'prices remained the same in the past year' (S_t) and 'prices went down in the past year' (F_t) we are left with the 'traditional' survey categories for which the CP-method was originally developed. The responses thus allow us to calculate the mean value of the perceived past inflation rate and the standard deviation of this rate, contingent on the form of the distribution function and a scaling factor representing a response threshold. The latter was chosen so as to equate the mean of the perceived past inflation rate with the mean of the actual past inflation rate.[9] This assumption differs from the one made by CP, where the unbiasedness assumption applied to expectations of future price developments. The latter assumption is especially problematic if the expectations data are to be used in tests of theories of expectations formation, such as the rational expectations hypothesis.

Before proceeding to the application of our method, some caveats should be mentioned. First, there is no reason why the response thresholds should be symmetric, as we assume. Second, the approach breaks down whenever a response category is equal to zero. Such a data point is not

[9] The implication is that the perceived inflation rate is an unbiased estimate of the actual inflation rate. However, this does not imply that the expected future inflation rate, which is the product of the perceived rate and a nonlinear term representing the frequencies of the assumed cumulative distribution function (see the Appendix), is by construction an unbiased estimate of the inflation rate.

admissable under continuous probability distributions. Third, the transformation of the original frequencies to a form which makes it possible to derive the moments of the assumed distribution is highly non-linear. The implication is that small sampling variations could produce large changes in the estimates of these distributional parameters. Fourth, it is assumed that the process of formation of the expected future inflation rate is independent of the formation of the perceived past inflation rate. Unclear is how restrictive this assumption is, and investigating the consequences of possible interactions seems an interesting topic for future research.

5.3 Empirical analysis

The empirical analysis is based on a sample of monthly data running from April 1986 up to and including February 1997.[10] We will distinguish between methods using a:

1. normal distribution (CPN);
2. symmetric scaled *t*-distribution (CPT);
3. noncentral scaled *t*-distribution, based on an asymmetry parameter using only information available to consumers when responding to the survey (CPAAT);
4. noncentral scaled t-distribution, based on an asymmetry parameter using information based on the entire sample (CPAST).

The symmetric distributions are calculated using both the lagged actual inflation rate (that is the most recent inflation figure available when responding to the survey) and the inflation rate which consumers perceived to have prevailed in the past 12 months as scaling parameters. The latter option was excluded for the asymmetric distributions, since it is not consistent with the assumptions on which the asymmetry parameter was based.

Table 5.1 presents some summary statistics of the various expectations measures. Labels ending with an 'O' indicate that the actual lagged inflation is used, as opposed to a 'P', which indicates that the perceived past inflation rate was used. It follows from the table that the expected inflation measures, with the exception of the central-*t* and normal distributions based on the actual inflation rate, show substantial bias. For example, the mean expected inflation based on the noncentral-*t* varied between 1.5% and 1.2%, where the actual 12-month-ahead-inflation rate

[10] The data are published in the Statistical Bulletin of the Dutch Central Bureau of Statistics or in European Economy, Supplement B, of the European Commission of the EC.

Table 5.1: Summary statistics for alternative measures of inflation expectations

Correlation	$\Pi(t+12)$	CPAATO	CPASTO	CPTO	CPTP	CPNO	CPNP
$\Pi(t+12)$	1.00						
CPAATO	0.47	1.00					
CPASTO	0.77	0.67	1.00				
CPTO	0.70	0.70	0.79	1.00			
CPTP	0.74	0.74	0.85	0.96	1.00		
CPNO	0.70	0.70	0.79	0.99	0.96	1.00	
CPNP	0.71	0.74	0.81	0.97	0.99	0.97	1.00
MEAN	2.05	1.52	1.17	1.78	1.45	1.78	1.47
STD DEV	1.12	1.75	1.13	1.58	0.99	1.58	1.05
RMSE		1.68	1.15	1.18	0.98	1.18	1.01
MAPE		1.37	0.97	0.94	0.81	0.94	0.85
THEIL1		0.72	0.50	0.51	0.42	0.51	0.44
THEIL2		6.53	4.47	4.59	3.80	4.59	3.93

Notes: Sample 1986:04-1997:02, n=116.

RMSE= Root Mean Square Prediction Error= $\sqrt{\frac{1}{n}\sum_{i=1}^{n}\left[\Pi(i+12)-\Pi^{e}(i)\right]^{2}}$

MAPE= Mean Absolute Prediction Error= $\frac{1}{n}\sum_{i=1}^{n}\left|\Pi(i+12)-\Pi^{e}(i)\right|$

THEIL1= Theils inequality coefficient= $\sqrt{\frac{\sum_{i=1}^{n}\left[\Pi(i+12)-\Pi^{e}(i)\right]^{2}}{\sum_{i=1}^{n}\left[\Pi(i+12)\right]^{2}}}$

THEIL2 is as THEIL1, with the denumerator replaced by $\sum_{i=1}^{n}\left[\Delta\Pi(i+12)\right]^{2}$

averaged 2.1%. From comparison of the summary statistics for the various distributions it follows that deviating from normal peakedness has no substantial effects (compare CPNO/CPNP with CPTO/CPTP), as opposed to deviating from symmetry (compare CPAATO/CPASTO with CPTO). This corroborates the findings of Batchelor (1986). The correlations between the various measures and the actual 12 month ahead inflation rate are in the 70%-75% range, with the exception of the CPAATO measure, which shows substantial less correlation. We next ranked the various expectations measures in order to conclude which measure has the highest accuracy relative to the other measures. We present the root mean squared prediction error (RMSE), the mean absolute prediction error (MAPE) and

Theils inequality coefficient as accuracy measures.[11] We computed two estimates of the Theil statistic, one to evaluate the predictive performance of the expected inflation measures with respect to a prediction of no change in the price level (THEIL1) and the other with respect to a prediction of equal change in the price level to what occurred in the month preceeding the date of the survey (THEIL2). Looking for minimal RMSE, MAPE, THEIL1 and THEIL2 gives us a ranking of expectation measures for each statistic. Averaging these rankings over the 4 available accuracy statistics gives the following score (from most accurate to least accurate): CPTP, CPNP, CPNO/CPTO, CPASTO and CPAATO. This leads us to the following conclusions. First, the measures based on symmetric distributions are more accurate than those based on noncentral-*t*. Second, using survey data on past price movements provides for more accurate expectations measures than using realised inflation figures. Third, there is little to choose between symmetric-*t* and normal distributions.

For THEIL1 as well as THEIL2, a value smaller (greater) than 1 implies that the predictive power of the expectations measure is better (worse) than the 'naive' forecast of a stable price level (THEIL1) or a constant inflation rate (THEIL2), respectively. Note the potentially disturbing finding that the values of THEIL2 exceed 1 for all expectations measures. This could be an indication of persistence of the inflation rate: if this rate follows an AR(1) process with parameter close to 1, the lagged inflation rate would be very informative with respect to the current inflation rate. This would explain the superiority of the naive forecast, as indicated by the values of THEIL2.

This last finding urges us to further investigate the issue of persistence. Insofar this persistence is due to nonstationarity of the (expected) inflation rate, it seems to be at odds with the method used to construct the expectations measures, which assumed constant first and second moments. However, even when the null hypothesis of a unit root can not be rejected this does not imply acceptance of an alternative of nonstationarity as the power of unit root tests is notoriously low against stationary alternatives with an autoregressive parameter close to unity (Campbell and Perron, 1991).[12] Moreover, our method is based on a *cross-sectional* sample of size N surveyed each month, so that the construction of the expected inflation measures is not influenced by possible persistence. The same, however, does not apply to the constructed *time series* of expected inflation rates.

---

[11] For a description of Theils inequality coefficient, see Koutsoyannis (1977, pp. 492-497).

[12] This point is especially important in our case because of the relatively short span of the sample period (1986:04-1997:02; 130 observations). This adversely affects the power of the unit root and the cointegration tests.

Table 5.2: Testing for nonstationarity

Number of unit roots	3	2	1
$\Pi(t+12)$	-7.23**	-5.13**	-1.21
CPAATO	-11.49**	-5.45**	-1.66
CPASTO	-11.57**	-6.06**	-2.00
CPTO	-11.15**	-4.42**	-1.19
CPTP	-10.46**	-4.91**	-0.78
CPNO	-11.03**	-3.81**	-1.88
CPNP	-10.38**	-4.84**	-0.60

Note: figures are values for the ADF test, with the number of lags as to ensure that the residuals are white noise.**= significant at 1%.

Table 5.2 presents the results of the integration analysis following the procedure recommended by Dickey and Pantula (1987), who emphasize the possibility of multiple unit roots. They show that first testing for *k* unit roots, and upon rejection proceeding with testing for *k-1* unit roots, and repeating this procedure until a null is accepted, ensures consistency. Table 2 overwhelmingly indicates that the inflation rate has a single unit root (that is, the price level is I(2)). The same applies to the measures of expected inflation. This has consequences for the admissable econometric strategy used in investigating the information content of expected inflation rates. Regressing actual inflation rates on expected inflation rates for example, as is done in the literature on the rationality of inflation expectations derived from survey data (see Pesaran, 1987, for an overview) would yield inconsistent parameter estimates, even when the covariance matrix is corrected parametrically to adjust for autocorrelation and heteroskedasticity.[13]

Given the high degree of persistence of the series under consideration, we next investigated the possibility that expected and actual future inflation rates are cointegrated. The concept of cointegration, which stresses long-term relationships, seems a suitable methodology given the orientation of monetary policymakers, who frequently stress the medium- to long-term horizons when striving for price stability (Bernanke and Mishkin, 1997). Cointegration implies that, although both the actual 12-month-ahead and expected inflation rates show substantial persistence and show no mean-reverting behaviour, both series form an equilibrium relationship in the sense that deviations from this relationship are

[13] Such a correction is necessary given the fact that the forecast horizon (in our study 12 months) exceeds the sampling interval (1 month in our case) (See Brown and Maital, 1981; Papadia, 1983). OLS in this case generates consistent parameter estimates, but inconsistent estimates of the covariance matrix, because, in violation of the classic OLS-assumptions, the disturbances are not serially uncorrelated but follow an MA(11) process. See Hansen and Hodrick (1980), Hansen (1982) and Hamilton (1994) for details.The Newey-West standard errors are asymptotically consistent in the presence of autocorrelation as well as heteroskedasticity.

temporary. This cointegrating relationship can, under certain additional conditions specified below, be of use for monetary policy purposes. Table 5.3 presents the results of the cointegration analysis, using the techniques developed by Johansen (see Johansen, 1995, for details).

Table 5.3: Testing for coïntegration

Coint between $\Pi(t+12)$ and:	Likelihood ratio test	coint vector
CPAATO	r=0 : LR=23.77* $r \leq 1$: LR= 4.60 *JB*= 6.47*	$\Pi(t+12) = \underset{(0.67)}{1.51}\, cpaato(t) - \underset{(1.51)}{1.05}$
CPASTO	r=0 : LR=33.97** $r \leq 1$: LR= 4.08 *JB*= 5.97*	$\Pi(t+12) = \underset{(0.10)}{1.24}\, cpasto(t) + \underset{(0.17)}{0.48}$
CPTO	r=0 : LR=24.81** $r \leq 1$: LR= 4.75 *JB*= 7.92*	$\Pi(t+12) = \underset{(0.10)}{0.77}\, cpto(t) + \underset{(0.24)}{0.55}$
CPTP	r=0 : LR=17.44 $r \leq 1$: LR= 6.37 *JB*= 1.33	--
CPNO	r=0 : LR=25.34** $r \leq 1$: LR= 4.79 *JB*= 7.70*	$\Pi(t+12) = \underset{(0.10)}{0.77}\, cpno(t) + \underset{(0.23)}{0.55}$
CPNP	r=0 : LR=17.10 $r \leq 1$: LR= 6.41 *JB*= 1.64	--

Note: r= number of cointegrating relations. ** (*) indicates significant at 1% (5%). Standard errors in parentheses. JB= Jarque-Bera normality test of the residuals from the vector error correction model on which the cointegration tests are based. The latter included 12 lags.

The likelihood ratio tests indicate that cointegration between the actual inflation rate 12 months ahead and the expected inflation rate can not be rejected for all measures except the ones based on the perceived inflation rate.[14] The lack of cointegration in the last case must be considered more important than the greater accuracy of the expectations measures based on the perceived inflation rate, because the latter finding could be spurious due

[14] Based on a visual inspection of the data, we decided against assuming deterministic trends in the data when constructing the VAR on which the likelihood ratio tests are based. The VAR included 12 lags.

to the persistence. Moreover, the greater accuracy is rather illusory, since all measures were outperformed by the naive forecast of a constant inflation rate.

The cointegration framework can be used to investigate the forecast consistency of inflation forecasts, as defined by Cheung and Chinn (1997). A forecast is consistent if it has a one-to-one relationship with future inflation in the long run (see also Fischer, 1989). This concept involves the behaviour of the forecast relative to the actual, over time and on average. The forecast consistency property implies that expected and future inflation (i) have the same order of integration, (ii) are cointegrated and (iii) have a cointegration vector $\Pi(t+12) = a + b\Pi^{e}(t)$ in which the restriction $a=0$, $b=1$ applies. It follows from tables 5.2 and 5.3 that the requirements (i) and (ii) are fulfilled for most expectation measures. We investigated restriction (iii) by testing for the existence of a unit root in the forecast error $\Pi(t+12) - \Pi^{e}(t)$, with the Augmented Dickey Fuller test implemented in a sequential manner as prescribed by Dickey and Pantula (1987).

The motivation for using this procedure instead of restricting the cointegrating vectors obtained by the Johansen procedure in table 5.3 is twofold. First, using the available prior information on the coefficients implies an efficiency gain in the procedures for investigating the time series properties of the data *vis-à-vis* not using this information. Second, the Johansen procedure assumes normality of the residuals. As indicated by table 3, the residuals from most of the equations do not pass the (Jarque-Bera) normality test. Huang and Yang (1996) conclude that the Engle-Granger method is more robust and dependable than the Johansen approach in the absence of normally distributed residuals. Investigating the stationarity of the forecast error implies implementing the Engle-Granger cointegration procedure, subject to the parameter restriction mentioned above. As can be seen from table 5.4, we could reject the null of 3, 2 and a single unit root for all measures of expected inflation forming a cointegrating relationship with future inflation, thereby confirming the rejection of non-cointegration implied by the Johansen procedure. Moreover, restriction (iii), which implies long-run unbiasedness of the inflation forecasts of consumers, therefore seems not to be refuted by the data. This is in line with the findings of Batchelor (1981) and Papadia (1983). It should be noted that the concept of forecast consistency focusses on the long-run property of forecasts, and hence is weaker than the one conventionally used in evaluating forecast rationality. It does not, for example, impose any further restrictions on the forecast errors, over-and-above the requirement that they be weakly covariance stationary.[15]

---

[15] In addition to unbiasedness, other necessary conditions for rationality include efficiency

Table 5.4: Testing for nonstationarity in the forecast error $\Pi(t+12)-\Pi^{e}(t)$

Number of unit roots	3	2	1
CPAATO	- 4.78**	-10.52**	-2.10*
CPASTO	-11.27**	-11.58**	-4.09**
CPTO	-11.42**	- 4.90**	-3.02*
CPNO	-11.32**	- 4.90**	-3.03*

Note: figures are values for the ADF test, with the number of lags as to ensure that the residuals are white noise.** (*)= significant at 1% (5%).

Cointegration merely implies the existence of a long-run relationship between, in this case, the actual 12-month-ahead inflation rate and expected inflation. It is well known (Engle and Granger, 1991) that cointegration per se does not provide information on the direction of causality in the long-term relationship. The normalization of the cointegrating vector on the inflation rate in table 5.3 is arbitrary. Yet the direction of causality in the cointegrating relationship between actual and expected inflation is of considerable importance for monetary policy. As will be discussed in the next paragraph, expected inflation must possess information content for the future inflation rate in order to be of use for monetary policy purposes. A statistical concept which is frequently used to measure this content is that of Granger causality. In addition to the traditional Granger causality tests, which consist of *F*-tests on exclusion restrictions in regressions of changes in the (expected) inflation rate, we investigated the issue of causality by analysing the vector error correction models on which the Johansen cointegration tests reported in table 5.3 are based. These models are VAR's which include an error correction term consisting of the lagged residual from cointegrating relations as in table 5.3. By Grangers Representation Theorem (Engle and Granger, 1987), the error correction terms provide additional information on the direction of causality.[16] The intuition is that if expected and actual inflation rates have a common stochastic trend, the current change in the latter rate is partly the result of the actual inflation rate moving into alignment with the trend value of the expected inflation rate. Given the normalization on the inflation rate in table 5.3, the expectation measure will Granger-cause the actual inflation rate if the error correction term is significant (as measured by conventional *t*-statistics) in

and orthogonality. Both conditions imply forecast errors that are, in general, not serially correlated. Empirical studies by and large reject the rationality of inflation expectations measures; see, for example, Batchelor and Dua (1987), Evans and Gulamani (1984), Holden and Peel (1977), Pesando (1975), De Menil and Bhalla (1975), De Leeuw and McKelvey (1981), Madsen (1996), Pearce (1979), Pesaran (1985), Thomas (1995) and Figlewski and Wachtel (1981).

[16] i.e. additional to the traditional Granger causality tests. Note that the latter should be formulated in terms of changes in (expected) inflation because of the persistence.

the equation for the inflation rate, but not in the equation for the expectation measure.

Table 5.5: Causality tests

Traditional Granger causality tests (F-statistic)	$\Delta\Pi^e$ does not cause $\Delta\Pi$	$\Delta\Pi$ does not cause $\Delta\Pi^e$
CPAATO	1.29	1.05
CPASTO	1.21	1.50
CPTO	1.46	1.86
CPTP	0.79	0.80
CPNO	1.43*	1.88*
CPNP	0.64	0.86
t-statistic of error correction term in VECM	**VECM for $\Delta\Pi(t+12)$**	**VECM for $\Delta\Pi^e(t)$**
CPAATO	1.06	-0.54
CPASTO	0.30	3.14**
CPTO	0.33	2.92**
CPTP	--	--
CPNO	0.32	2.96**
CPNP	--	--

Note: VECM and traditional Granger causality test include 12 lags of $\Delta\Pi(t)$ and $\Delta\Pi^e(t)$.** (*) indicates significant at 1%(5%).

It follows from table 5.5 that the traditional Granger causality tests do not reject the hypotheses of no causality in either direction (with the possible exception of the CPTO measure, in which case the evidence, however, is not very strong). The statistics based on the significance of the error correction terms uniformly indicate that the hypothesis that causality runs from actual inflation to the expected inflation rate could not be rejected. The evidence therefore seems to indicate that the expectations measures do not have predictive power for actual future inflation.

5.4 The usefulness of directly estimated expected inflation measures for monetary policy

Dutch monetary policy was until the start of stage 3 of EMU in January 1999 oriented towards maintaining an exchange rate peg with the D-Mark. As a consequence of this policy, Dutch and German price levels are cointegrated, and the Netherlands imports the relatively low German inflation rate (Berk and Winder, 1994). However, such an exchange rate target is not a viable option for the monetary policy which is conducted by the European Central Bank in Stage Three of EMU (EMI, 1997).[17] Possible

[17] In a relatively closed economy such as the euro-area, the benefit of exchange rate stability vis-a-vis a major trading partner (such as the US) would not outweigh the costs of losing one's ability to tailor monetary policy specifically to domestic economic conditions. Given a

candidates for a monetary policy strategy of the European Central Bank include intermediate monetary targeting and direct inflation targeting (DIT).[18] DIT is a framework for conducting monetary policy in which decisions are guided by expectations of future inflation relative to the announced inflation target. In a direct inflation targeting strategy, the monetary policymaker announces a target or a target range for future inflation. A change in the current policy stance is desirable if projected inflation over a medium-term horizon falls outside the announced range. Thus, in contrast to its name, DIT is in fact an intermediate targeting procedure, where the expected inflation rate, as measured by projected inflation, functions as an intermediate target (Svensson, 1996). The expected inflation rate therefore is an essential element of the DIT strategy (Debelle, 1997). Possible candidates for expected inflation include forecasts from large scale macroeconometric models, forecasts from time series models (such as VAR's), or direct measures obtained from financial market indicators (such as yield curves) or from surveys. Measures of inflation expectations derived from survey data are not under control of the monetary authority, which precludes using them as an intermediate target. In order to be of value as an information variable, there needs to be a stable statistical relationship between expected and future actual inflation, where the latter is conventionally measured in terms of official price statistics such as the CPI (Sijben, 1977; 1995).[19] Our finding that current inflation expectations and future realisations are cointegrated, and that the forecast error is stationary, confirms the usefulness of the former as an information variable for monetary policy: expected inflation derived from consumer surveys shows an identical long-run behaviour to the actual inflation 12 months ahead. But, our analysis also showed a drawback to this indicator: the expectations of Dutch consumers concerning future price movements show no causal relationship with future inflation. This implies that it would be inadvisable to use feedback rules from the indicator of consumer inflation expectations when setting monetary policy.[20] We have shown that the indicators studied in this chapter do not derive their usefulness in forecasting future inflation from being (proxies of) causal determinants of inflation. The connection between the underlying sources of inflationary pressure (that monetary policy wants to respond to) and the indicator is channeled primarily through expectations. In that case it is most plausible

---

relatively closed economy, exchange rate stability would not provide firm assurances for price stability.

[18] For a recent discussion of this topic, see King (1996), Green (1996), Bernanke and Mishkin (1997).

[19] These are the basic concepts of stability and predictability for evaluating information variables; see Shigehara (1996) for details.

[20] For a related discussion on the mechanics of implementing inflation targeting in practice, see Baumgartner, Ramaswamy and Zettergren (1997).

that the relation will radically change in the case of a policy intervention that modifies the relation between the underlying states and the inflation that eventually occurs (Woodford, 1994).

5.5 Concluding Remarks

In this chapter we developed and analysed measures of expected future inflation extracted from consumer surveys in the Netherlands. In these qualitative surveys respondents were asked questions regarding past and future price developments. Six different response categories were allowed for each question. This setup made it possible to develop a variant of the Carlson-Parkin (1977) probability method which generated time-varying response thresholds and did not assume unbiased forecasts. Instead, the expected inflation rate was scaled with the perceived past inflation rate, for which either the actual inflation rate available to respondents when answering the survey, or the information derived from the survey question regarding past price developments was used. The latter improved the accuracy of expectations measures relative to the former. We based our probability measures on normal, central and noncentral t-distributions, and concluded that allowing for nonnormal peakedness and asymmetry did not improve the accuracy of the expected inflation measures. We showed that the actual inflation rate as well as the expected inflation measures were nonstationary, and in most cases were cointegrated. The finding that currently observed inflation expectations of consumers and the unobserved 12-months ahead inflation rate have identical long-run properties is of interest for policymakers. But making use of this long-term relationship for monetary policy purposes, for example in the direct inflation targeting strategy of monetary policy, seems hazardous. This is because the expectations measures are not causal determinants of future inflation.

Appendix to chapter 5

1 *Calculating the expected future inflation rate from survey responses*
Our method is based on the following assumptions, which are an extension of those developed by Pesaran (1987) and Visco (1984). Below we define $cpi_{i,t}$ and $cpi_{i,t}^{p}$ as the actual and perceived level of the consumer price index relevant for consumer *i*, respectively. The actual future and perceived past inflation rates relevant for consumer *i* are denoted as $\Pi_{i,t+12} = \ln(cpi_{i,t+12}) - \ln(cpi_{i,t})$ and $\Pi_{it}^{p} = \ln(cpi_{it}^{p}) - \ln(cpi_{i,t-12}^{p})$, respectively.

Assumption I. Each consumer *i* bases its survey response on a subjective, time invariant conditional probability distribution of future inflation outcomes $h_i(\Pi_{i,t+12}|\Phi_{it})$ where Φ_{it} represents the information set available at time t.

Assumption II. A consumer reports that he expects prices to remain the same in the coming 12 months if: $|{}_t\Pi_{i,t+12}^{e}| < \varepsilon \forall i$ and ε is any positive scalar.

Assumption III. A consumer reports that he expects the price rise to remain unchanged in the coming 12 months if the rise lies within an interval centered on the currently perceived inflation rate : $\Pi_{it}^{p} - \delta \leq {}_t\Pi_{i,t+12}^{e} \leq \Pi_{it}^{p} + \delta$. These δ is any positive scalar.

Assumption IV. The perceived inflation rate is fixed among consumers, i.e. $\Pi_{it}^{p} = \Pi_{t}^{p}\ \forall i$. This perceived rate is assumed known or can be estimated independently from the procedures used to estimate the future inflation rate.

Assumption V. The subjective distributions of consumers $h_i(\Pi_{i,t+12}|\Phi_{it})$ are such that they can be employed to derive an 'aggregate' probability distribution $h(\Pi_{t+12}|\Omega_t)$ with finite first and second-order moments, where $\Omega_t = \bigcup_{i=1}^{N} \Phi_{it}$ is the union of individual consumers' information sets and $\Pi_{t+12} = \sum_{i=1}^{N} w_i \Pi_{i,t+12}$, in which Π_{t+12} denotes the actual future percentage change in consumer prices, and w_i are the weights of products bought by consumer i in domestic product.

Assumption VI. The subjective probability distributions

$h_i\left(\Pi_{i,t+12} | \Phi_{it}\right)$ are independent and have the same known form across consumers.[21] It is also assumed to possess finite first and second moments.

Assumptions V and VI ensure that ${}_t\Pi^e_{i,t+12}$ can be regarded as independent drawings from the 'aggregate' distribution. Assumptions II, and III specify the form of the response function of consumers, relating their qualitative responses to the underlying quantitative changes in their expectations. Note that, in contrast to the original CP-method, our variant allows for time-varying thresholds. See Seitz (1988) and Smith and MacAleer (1990) for an empirical corroboration of the assumption of time varying thresholds.[22]

Now define the variable Z as:

$$Z_{t+12} = \frac{\Pi_{t+12} - {}_t\Pi^e_{t+12}}{\sigma_{t+12}} \tag{A}$$

that is the future inflation rate is transformed by subtracting its mean and dividing the result by the standard deviation of the expected inflation rate (the so-called Z-score). Given assumptions I-VI, and denoting the cumulative density function of $h\left(\Pi_{t+12} | \Omega_t\right)$ as $H_t(.)$, we can write

$$\begin{aligned} {}_tRR^e_{t+12} &= prob\left(Z_{t+12} \geq Z^1_{t+12} | \Omega_t\right) = \int_{Z^1_{t+12}}^{\infty} h\left(Z_{t+12} | \Omega_t\right) dZ_{t+12} = \\ &= 1 - H_t\left(Z^1_{t+12}\right) \end{aligned} \tag{B}$$

$$\begin{aligned} {}_tER^e_{t+12} &= prob\left(Z^2_{t+12} \leq Z_{t+12} \leq Z^1_{t+12} | \Omega_t\right) = \int_{Z^2_{t+12}}^{Z^1_{t+12}} h\left(Z_{t+12} | \Omega_t\right) dZ_{t+12} = \\ &= H_t\left(Z^1_{t+12}\right) - H_t\left(Z^2_{t+12}\right) \end{aligned} \tag{C}$$

$$\begin{aligned} {}_tWR^e_{t+12} &= prob\left(Z^3_{t+12} \leq Z_{t+12} \leq Z^2_{t+12} | \Omega_t\right) = \int_{Z^3_{t+12}}^{Z^2_{t+12}} h\left(Z_{t+12} | \Omega_t\right) dZ_{t+12} = \\ &= H_t\left(Z^2_{t+12}\right) - H_t\left(Z^3_{t+12}\right) \end{aligned} \tag{D}$$

---

[21] See Figlewski and Wachtel (1981) on the effects of differences of expectations between individuals.

[22] These authors estimate time varying thresholds within a traditional CP-framework with a model of stochastic parameter variation proposed by Cooley and Prescott (1976).

$$ {}_tC^e_{t+12} = prob\left(Z^4_{t+12} \le Z_{t+12} \le Z^3_{t+12} | \Omega_t\right) = \int_{Z^4_{t+12}}^{Z^3_{t+12}} h\left(Z_{t+12} | \Omega_t\right) dZ_{t+12} = H_t\left(Z^3_{t+12}\right) - H_t\left(Z^4_{t+12}\right) \tag{E} $$

$$ {}_tF^e_{t+12} = prob\left(Z_{t+12} \le Z^4_{t+12} | \Omega_t\right) = \int_{-\infty}^{Z^4_{t+12}} h\left(Z_{t+12} | \Omega_t\right) dZ_{t+12} = H_t\left(Z^4_{t+12}\right) \tag{F} $$

where:

$$ Z^1_{t+12} = \frac{\Pi^p_t + \delta_t - {}_t\Pi^e_{t+12}}{\sigma_{t+12}} \tag{G} $$

$$ Z^2_{t+12} = \frac{\Pi^p_t - \delta_t - {}_t\Pi^e_{t+12}}{\sigma_{t+12}} \tag{H} $$

$$ Z^3_{t+12} = \frac{\varepsilon_t - {}_t\Pi^e_{t+12}}{\sigma_{t+12}} \tag{I} $$

$$ Z^4_{t+12} = \frac{-\varepsilon_t - {}_t\Pi^e_{t+12}}{\sigma_{t+12}} \tag{J} $$

${}_tRR^e_{t+12}$ is the proportion of consumers surveyed at time t that expect prices to rise faster over the next 12 months, ${}_tER^e_{t+12}$ is the proportion of consumers that at time t expect prices in the coming 12 months to rise at a rate comparable to the past 12 months, ${}_tWR^e_{t+12}$ is the proportion that expect prices to rise less strongly in the coming 12 months,, ${}_tC^e_{t+12}$ is the proportion expecting prices to remain unchanged in the coming 12 months and ${}_tF^e_{t+12}$ is the proportion that expect prices to fall in the coming year. The relationship between the observed fractions RR, ER, WR, C and F and the transformed variables Z can be seen to be dependent on the form of the cumulative distribution function H:[23]

$$ Z^1_{t+12} = H^{-1}_t\left(1 - {}_tRR^e_{t+12}\right) \tag{K} $$

$$ Z^2_{t+12} = H^{-1}_t\left(1 - {}_tRR^e_{t+12} - {}_tER^e_{t+12}\right) \tag{L} $$

$$ Z^3_{t+12} = H^{-1}_t\left(1 - {}_tRR^e_{t+12} - {}_tER^e_{t+12} - {}_tWR^e_{t+12}\right) \tag{M} $$

$$ Z^4_{t+12} = H^{-1}_t\left({}_tF^e_{t+12}\right) \tag{N} $$

[23] Only four of the five possible response categories are independent because the total of the proporties must equal 1.

Rearranging equations (G)-(J) gives us the following expressions:

$$\frac{{}_t\Pi^e_{t+12}}{\Pi^p_t} = -\frac{Z^3_{t+12} + Z^4_{t+12}}{Z^1_{t+12} + Z^2_{t+12} - Z^3_{t+12} - Z^4_{t+12}} \tag{O}$$

$$\frac{\sigma_{t+12}}{\Pi^p_t} = \frac{2}{Z^1_{t+12} + Z^2_{t+12} - Z^3_{t+12} - Z^4_{t+12}} \tag{P}$$

$$\frac{\delta_t}{\Pi^p_t} = \frac{Z^1_{t+12} - Z^2_{t+12}}{Z^1_{t+12} + Z^2_{t+12} - Z^3_{t+12} - Z^4_{t+12}} \tag{Q}$$

$$\frac{\varepsilon_t}{\Pi^p_t} = \frac{Z^3_{t+12} - Z^4_{t+12}}{Z^1_{t+12} + Z^2_{t+12} - Z^3_{t+12} - Z^4_{t+12}} \tag{R}$$

Equations (O)-(R) are the solutions for the 4 unknowns in the system, i.e. the mean and standard deviation of the future inflation rate as well as the response thresholds, all scaled with respect to the perceived inflation rate.

2 Probability method based on a t-distribution
Praetz (1972) showed that changes in share prices can be best represented by the following scaled symmetrical *t*-distribution:

$$t^i_{t+12} = \left(\frac{n}{n-2}\right)^{0.5} Z^i_{t+12} \overset{d}{=} t(n) \tag{S}$$

where i=1,2,3,4.

With this transformation the system (K)-(N) can be written as:

$$\psi Z^1_{t+12} = \Gamma^{-1}_t\left(1 - {}_tRR^e_{t+12}\right) \tag{T}$$

$$\psi Z^2_{t+12} = \Gamma^{-1}_t\left(1 - {}_tRR^e_{t+12} - {}_tER^e_{t+12}\right) \tag{U}$$

$$\psi Z^3_{t+12} = \Gamma^{-1}_t\left(1 - {}_tRR^e_{t+12} - {}_tER^e_{t+12} - {}_tWR^e_{t+12}\right) \tag{V}$$

$$\psi Z^4_{t+12} = \Gamma^{-1}_t\left({}_tF^e_{t+12}\right) \tag{W}$$

with $\psi = \left(\frac{n}{n-2}\right)^{0.5}$ and $\Gamma^{-1}_t(.)$ the abscissa of the frequencies of the central *t*-distribution. As can be easily verified, the solutions are similar to those presented in (O)-(R), with the Z^i_{t+12} replaced by the t^i_{t+12}. The exception is the solution for the standard deviation, which now becomes:

$$\frac{\sigma_{t+12}}{\Pi_t^p} = \frac{2\psi}{t_{t+12}^1 + t_{t+12}^2 - t_{t+12}^3 - t_{t+12}^4} \qquad \text{(X)}$$

The analytic expressions for the solutions under the noncentral-*t* distributions are similar to those mentioned above.

6 PRICE MOVEMENTS IN THE NETHERLANDS AND GERMANY AND THE GUILDER- DMARK PEG[1]

6.1 Introduction

Dutch monetary policy was until the start of stage three of EMU in January 1999 aimed at maintaining a stable exchange rate of the guilder *vis-à-vis* the German mark. The ultimate objective was an inflation rate which is in line with the relatively low inflation rate in Germany. A credible exchange rate policy, moreover, lead to a low interest rate differential with Germany through mitigation of uncertainties and consequently a lower risk premium in Dutch interest rates. In this way monetary policy contributed to non-inflationary, steady economic growth. Naturally, a well-balanced fiscal policy and modest wage increases were also crucial to achive price stability. In addition to a direct effect, the guilder - Dmark peg also had an indirect influence by means of its disciplinating effect on the government's behaviour and that of the employers' organizations and trade unions.

The primary objective of this chapter is to examine the relationship between Dutch and German prices and, more specifically, whether the policy conducted has resulted in similar price movements in the two countries. Section 2 discusses the theoretical framework and the hypotheses to be examined, while section 3 gives the empirical results. Concluding remarks are presented in section 4.

6.2 Theoretical framework

The ultimate objective of the Dutch exchange rate policy was that Dutch and German inflation rates move in line. It was therefore not necessary that these rates should be exactly the same every year. Inflation rate differentials should rather initiate adjustment processes to restore equilibrium, thus ensuring that perturbations are only temporary. In view of the high degree of integration between the Netherlands and Germany, diverging prices will initiate changes in the current account, the profitability of enterprises and the unemployment situation. This will affect wage negotiations and expenditures and consequently also the prices (see Wellink, 1990).

For the analysis of the relationship between Dutch and German prices in the longer term - i.e. abstracting from temporary divergences - use is

[1] Reprinted from, *De Economist*, 142 (1), (1994), J.M. Berk and C.C.A. Winder, "Price Movements in the Netherlands and Germany and the guilder – Dmark Peg", 63-74 .© 1994 with kind permission from Kluwer Academic Publishers.

made of (co)integration techniques. They enable us to examine the long-term properties of economic variables in a simple manner. For a detailed discussion of the conceptual framework we refer to Engle and Granger (1991).

Consider a price variable P for which the following model is postulated

$$\ln(P_t) = \alpha_0 + \alpha_1\, tr_t + \varepsilon_t \tag{1}$$

where tr is a deterministic trend variable, t the time index, α_0 and α_1 constant parameters and ε_t a disturbance term. No specific requirements are imposed on ε_t. For instance, ε_t, which corresponds with the detrended price, may be autocorrelated. The study focuses solely on the long-run properties of P. These properties are characterized by the order of integration of the deviations of $ln\ (P_t)$ from its deterministic path (see also Nelson and Plosser, 1982). If ε_t follows a stationary process, or in other words is integrated of order 0, the price variable is called trend-stationary. If, on the other hand, ε_t is integrated of order 1 - i.e. if $\Delta\varepsilon_t \equiv \varepsilon_t - \varepsilon_{t-1}$ is stationary - the price level is difference-stationary. In the former case, deviations from the deterministic growth path are only temporary. Hence, an error correcting mechanism is present. In the latter case, this mechanism is absent, causing a shock to have a permanent effect on the future price level.

As monetary policy is generally formulated in terms of *inflation*, we briefly discuss the effects for the inflation process. From (1) it follows that

$$\Delta \ln(P_t) = \alpha_1 + \Delta\varepsilon_t \tag{2}$$

If the price level is difference-stationary, a one-time perturbation will lead to a temporary deviation of the *inflation rate* from the its equilibrium value α_1. If, on the other hand, the price series is trend-stationary, the same initial deviation of the inflation rate will occur, but -due to the adjustment processes that induce the price level's return to its deterministic trend - it will be followed in the next periods by an adjustment with the opposite sign. If ε_t follows a white noise process, the deviations in the two subsequent periods have the same size but opposite sign. In both the difference- and trend-stationary case, however, the effect of a price shock on the inflation rate is only temporary.

Using the above, two hypotheses concerning the price movements in The Netherlands and Germany can be formulated. Define, by analogy with (1), the following processes for the Dutch (*Pnl*) and German price levels (*Pge*):

$$\ln(Pnl_t) = \alpha_0 + \alpha_1 tr_t + \varepsilon_t \tag{3}$$

$$\ln(Pge_t) = \beta_0 + \beta_1 tr_t + \mu_t \tag{4}$$

For the difference between Dutch and German price levels and the inflation rate differential, we have respectively

$$\ln(Pnl_t / Pge_t) = \alpha_0 - \beta_0 + (\alpha_1 - \beta_1)\, tr_t + \varepsilon_t - \mu_t \tag{5}$$

and

$$\Delta \ln(Pnl_t) - \Delta \ln(Pge_t) = \alpha_1 - \beta_1 + \Delta(\varepsilon_t - \mu_t) \tag{6}$$

The first hypothesis concerns the ultimate objective of the guilder-Dmark peg: a Dutch inflation rate which, apart from temporary deviations, equals the German inflation rate. Equation (6) shows that - provided that the order of integration of the price variables does not exceed 1, $\alpha_1 = \beta_1$ is a necessary and sufficient condition. This restriction implies that the prices in The Netherlands and in Germany have the same trendlike behaviour. Consequently, the inflation rates in both countries are - ignoring temporary divergences - identical.

The second hypothesis to be examined is whether Dutch and German price levels are cointegrated. This requires that the individual prices are difference-stationary, whereas the Dutch-German price ratio is trend-stationary[2]. In terms of the above equations, this means that ε_t and μ_t are integrated of order 1 but that $\varepsilon_t - \mu_t$ follows a stationary process. Hence, a perturbation has a permanent effect on the future price both in The Netherlands and in Germany, but the implied deviation in the relative price ratio is temporary. The economic interpretation of this second hypothesis is that the change in the Dutch competitiveness *vis-à-vis* Germany, which *ceteris paribus* is the result from a price shock in the Netherlands differing from that in Germany, will be corrected.

Notice that cointegration only concerns the properties of the

---

[2] Trend-stationarity of the relative price ratio implies cointegration between Dutch and German prices levels, with a cointegrating vector of (1-1)'.

deviations from the deterministic path. If the slope coefficients α_1 and β_1 in (3) and (4) differ, the ratio of the prices will display a deterministic trend. Therefore, even if cointegration occurs, the Dutch competitiveness will improve or deteriorate systematically *vis-à-vis* Germany. If both the first and the second hypothesis are valid, the above change in competitiveness is fully compensated for. Suppose that the structural inflation rate, both in Germany and in The Netherlands, is 3%. A perturbation in the Netherlands, resulting in a one-time 1 percentage point increase in the Dutch inflation rate, will - assuming that the adjustments take place immediately - lead to a Dutch inflation rate in the next period of 2%, in order to offset the loss of competitiveness inflicted in the first period. Thus, the divergence between the inflation rates is not only eliminated, but even offset.

The above discussion shows that cointegration is not a necessary condition for the Dutch inflation rate to move in line with the German inflation rate, since cointegration may also occur when Dutch and German price show diverging trends $(\alpha_1 \neq \beta_1)$. Cointegration is neither a sufficient condition for the ultimate objective of Dutch monetary policy to be realised, since rejection of the hypothesis of cointegration is compatible with identical long-run inflation rates, provided that the restriction $\alpha_1 = \beta_1$ applies. This follows from the fact that, if $\varepsilon_t - \mu_t$ is integrated of order 1, the disturbance term in (6) will still follow a stationary process.

If the price variables are difference-stationary, each individual perturbation has a permanent effect on the future course of the prices. However, it may also be the case that not all perturbations have a permanent effect, but only some important ones - such as, within the context of the present study, the establisment of the EMS or the reorientation in Dutch exchange rate policy[3] - do. Perron (1989) discusses the implications and required adjustments of the standard test procedures if the constant and/or trend coefficient in (1) is subject to stuctural changes. These changes represent the permanent perturbations.

In the next section, it will be argued that as a result of the establishment of the EMS, the trend coefficient in (1) has changed.[4] In the

[3] The moment when the peg between the guilder and the Dmark began to serve as a policy objective *grosso modo* coincides with that of the establishment of the EMS. As Van der Wal (1991) notes in his general description of the evolution of Dutch exchange rate policy, the shift in policy has been a gradual one. After the realignment of the EMS currencies in September 1979, the confidence aspect of a hard guilder is explicitly mentioned. *De facto*, however, the guilder-Dmark peg had already been an objective of monetary policy for some time before the establishment of the EMS.

[4] With the establishment of the EMS, the volatility of the deviations from the deterministic path could have changed as well. Graphical inspection, however, does not indicate that this has occurred. In the empirical analysis, it is therefore assumed that the sole effect of the introduction of the EMS was a structural change in the trend coefficient.

empirical analysis, the following model is examined

$$\ln(Pnl_t) = \alpha_0 + \alpha_1 tr1_t + \alpha_2 tr2_t + \varepsilon_t \tag{7}$$

$$\ln(Pge_t) = \beta_0 + \beta_1 tr1_t + \beta_2 tr2_t + \mu_t \tag{8}$$

where *tr1* is a trend variable for the pre-EMS period and *tr2* a trend variable for the period following the establishment of the EMS. For the individual sub-periods, (7) and (8) are identical to (3) and (4). Therefore, the above discussion remains valid for the model with structural change. However, the hypothesis concerning the objective of Dutch exchange rate policy is only relevant for the EMS period, since before March 1979 the co-movement of German and Dutch inflation rates was not an explicit policy objective. The hypotheses to be examined in the following section are therefore: a) equal trendlike behaviour of the Dutch and German prices during the EMS period $(\alpha_2 = \beta_2)$ and b) cointegration between the prices in the two countries (ε_t and μ_t integrated of order 1 and ε_t - μ_t stationary).

The analysis could be restricted to only those data that refer to the EMS period. With such a relatively short time span the power of the tests may be quite low (see also Perron, 1989). This may be reflected in mutually conflicting results. The empirical results - extensively discussed in the next section - serve as an illustration. Considering data for the EMS period only, the evidence suggests that both Dutch and German prices are trend-stationary. Since a linear combination of stationary variables is stationary, the ratio of Dutch and German prices should be trend-stationary. The test statistics, however, indicate that the price ratio is difference-stationary. Including pre-1979 data eliminates this inconsistency and has the further advantage that the results obtained for the periods before and after the establishment of the EMS can be compared.

6.3 Empirical results

This section discusses the results of the empirical analysis of monthly data on Dutch and German consumer prices for the period 1961:1-1991:12. The price series are those which the monetary authorities consider as most relevant.[5] The methodology discussed in the previous section has been

[5] The Dutch consumer price index is the 'prijsindex gezinsconsumptie, reeks werknemers gezinnen met een gezinsinkomen beneden de loongrens van de ziekenfondsverzekering, 1985 = 100' (cost-of-living index (1985 = 100) for households with an income below the upper limit for compulsory Health Insurance). It is published by the Central Bureau of Statistics in the Statistical Bulletin. For Germany, the consumer price index refers to West Germany only. The series used is the 'Preisindex (1985 = 100) für die Lebenshaltung aller privaten

applied to the individual Dutch and German price series as well as to the Dutch-German price ratio. The latter refers to the price competitiveness between the Netherlands and Germany, as measured by consumer prices. Generally, only prices relating to tradeables such as industrial output prices are used to measure price competitiveness. However, from the point of view of policy relevance, consumer prices are more interesting as they are commonly used to formulate inflation rate objectives.

First, the data have been analysed without explicitly allowing for structural changes. In this analysis, the results of which are summarized in the Appendix, we considered both the entire sample period 1961-1991 and the EMS period individually. The results pertaining to the EMS period are mutually inconsistent. The individual price series are found to be trend-stationary. Therefore, the same conclusion should follow for the relative price ratio. The empirical results, however, indicate that the ratio between Dutch and German prices is difference-stationary. This result illustrates the risks attached to the application of the methodology to time series covering a relatively short time span, as mentioned in the previous section. For the whole sample period, the empirical analysis does yield mutually consistent results. Both the individual price series and the relative price ratio are found to be difference-stationary. The conclusion might therefore be that Dutch and German prices are not cointegrated and that perturbations have a permanent effect on the relative price ratio between the two countries. However, Perron (1989) proved that one single perturbation may be responsible for this finding. The correct interpretation of the estimation results is therefore that at least one permanent perturbation has occurred. The standard procedures cannot discriminate between situations in which each individual price shock has a permanent influence and situations in which only one important perturbation has a permanent effect.

Graphic inspection of the data provides information with respect to the possibility that a structural change has occurred and if so, when it has taken place. Figure 6.1 depicts therefore the - logarithmically transformed - Dutch-German price ratio. It clearly indicates a structural change during the late 1970s. During the first part of the sample period the relative price ratio shows a strong increase. This reflects the fact that Dutch prices systematically rose stronger than the German ones. In the 1980s the price ratio between the two countries is nearly constant. Obviously, Dutch and German prices have the same trendlike behaviour during this period. In view of these findings, the assumption of an exogenous structural change in 1979:3, relating to the establishment of the EMS and the reorientation in the

---

Haushalte'. It is published by the Statistisches Bundesamt and is obtained from the 'Monatsberichte der Deutschen Bundesbank'.

Figure 6.1: Dutch-German price ratio, 1961-1991

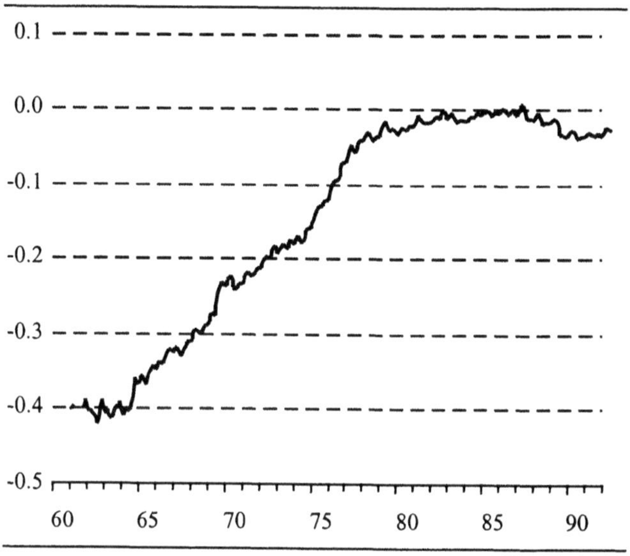

exchange rate policy of the Nederlandsche Bank, is made and explicity incorporated in the analysis. The procedure developed by Perron (1989) to test for (co)integration in case structural changes are present, which will be applied below to the two individual price series and the ratio of both prices, can be summarized as follows. Assuming that the variable to be examined is x_t, the following equation is estimated:

$$x_t = \beta + \gamma_1 tr1_t + \gamma_2 tr2_2 + \varepsilon_t \tag{9}$$

where $tr1_t$ and $tr2_t$ are trend variables for the periods before and after the establishment of the EMS:

$tr1 =$	t	1961(1)-1979(3)	$tr2 =$	0	1961(1)-1979(3)
	219	1979(4)-1991(12)		t-219	1979(4)-1991(12)

Subsequently, the order of integration of the residuals e_t is examined with the following equation:

$$\Delta e_t = \rho\, e_{t-1} + \mu_t \tag{10}$$

The null hypothesis of difference-stationarity can be tested using the t-ratio of $\hat{\rho}$ $(t(\hat{\rho}))$ or $T\hat{\rho}$, where T represents the number of observations. These statistics do not have the conventional distributions. Perron (1989) derives the correct asymptotic distributions and tabulates the critical values, which are determined by means of simulation experiments. These critical values may be used provided that μ_t in (10) is white noise. If μ_t shows autocorrelation, lags of Δe_t have to be included as additional explanatory variables. In the present study we estimated equation (10), expanded with the first twelve lags of Δe_t, and successively eliminated the most insignificant one of these lags, so that in the resulting final equation only significant lags of Δe_t occur. The results obtained for the three series considered are summarized in Table 6.1.

Table 6.1: Estimation results

Variable	$\hat{\gamma}_1$	$\hat{\gamma}_2$	$t(\hat{\rho})$	$T\hat{\rho}$
ln(Pnl)	0.0055 (120.06)	0.0025 (36.35)	-2.38	-5.27
ln(Pge)	0.0035 (92.51)	0.0025 (43.82)	-3.26	-3.94
ln(Pnl/Pge)	0.0020 (146.19)	0.0000 (0.02)	-4.41	-35.15
ln(Pnl/Pge)	0.0020 (181.99)	-	-4.41	-35.15

Note: The figures in parentheses are *t*-values. At a level of significance of 0.05, critical values of $t(\hat{\rho})$ and $T\hat{\rho}$ are -3.96 and -29.52, respectively.

For the trend coefficient during the EMS period a highly significant value of 0.0025 is found for both the Dutch and German prices. In view of these results, it is to be expected that the estimate of this coefficient in the equation of the Dutch-German price ratio is nil and not significant. Estimating equation (9) for the price ratio yields the results in the third line of Table 1, which confirm this intitution. Imposing the restriction that during the EMS period the trend coefficient in the equation of the relative price ratio is equal to zero does not affect the estimates of the other parameters. These results constitute empirical support for the first hypothesis formulated in the preceding section. During the EMS period Dutch and German prices show the same trendlike behaviour, and hence the objective of the exchange rate policy has been achieved. Of course, the modest wage increases in this period and the government's fiscal policy (notably in the second half of the 1980s) also contributed to these price movements. Insofar as the behaviour of employers' organizations, trade unions and the government was the result of the disciplinary effect of the exchange rate policy conducted, this can be considered as an indirect effect of the guilder-Dmark peg.

The second hypothesis formulated in the preceding section - cointegration between Dutch and German prices - cannot be rejected either. The results in Table 6.1 indicate that the individual prices are difference-stationary, but that the relative price ratio is trend-stationary. This conclusion follows for both the model with and without the restriction that the trend coefficient during the EMS period is equal to zero. Comparison with results obtained earlier in the analysis that did not allow for the single trend break, indicates that only the structural change as a result of the establishment of the EMS has had a permanent effect on the Dutch-German price ratio. The other perturbations only had temporary effects. This conclusion does not apply to the individual price variables. The fact that cointegration is not rejected, implies that Dutch economic agents monitor the German price movements closely. For example, in wage negotiations in Dutch industry considerable importance is attached to the corresponding outcome in Germany. This is because a Dutch wage increase which exceeds the one in Germany - *ceteris paribus* - has adverse effects on sales and, ultimately, employment.

The robustness of the results found with respect to the relationship between Dutch and German prices is examined in more detail with the following generalisation of the final equation obtained in the foregoing analysis:

$$\ln(Pnl_t) = \phi \ln(Pge_t) + \beta + \gamma_1 tr1_t + \varepsilon_t \qquad (11)$$

with γ_1 corresponding to the difference between the slope coefficients for the Dutch and German prices during the pre-EMS period. In the previous analysis it was assumed *a priori* that ϕ is equal to 1 and the question arises whether this restriction is justifiable. For an assessment of the ultimate objective of exchange rate policy this is a crucial assumption, as the inflation rate in The Netherlands will deviate systematically from that in Germany if ϕ is not equal to 1. When assessing the validity of this restriction, a problem is that the conventional estimation and testing theory does not apply if the price variables are difference-stationary (see e.g. Stock, 1987). Hence, the restriction $\phi = 1$ cannot be tested formally. However, if Dutch and German prices are cointegrated, the OLS estimator of ϕ in (11) is consistent and the order of magnitude of $\hat{\phi}$ gives an indication as to whether the restriction $\phi = 1$ is valid. Estimation of (11) gives

$$\ln(Pnl_t) = \underset{(139.81)}{1.0264} \ln(Pge_t) - \underset{(20.82)}{0.5405} + \underset{(53.68)}{0.0019}\, tr1_t \qquad (12)$$

with conventional *t*-ratios in parentheses. To examine the order of integration of the residuals from (12), equation (10), expanded with significant lags of the first differences, was estimated. This resulted in a *t*-ratio for $\hat{\rho}$ of -4.39 and and a value of -35.20 for $T\hat{\rho}$. Comparison with the critical values determined by Perron leads - as before - to the conclusion that Dutch and German prices are cointegrated. Moreover, the estimate of ϕ is close to 1, implying that the results in Table 6.1 gain in reliability.

Figure 6.2: Recursive estimates ϕ, 1961-1991

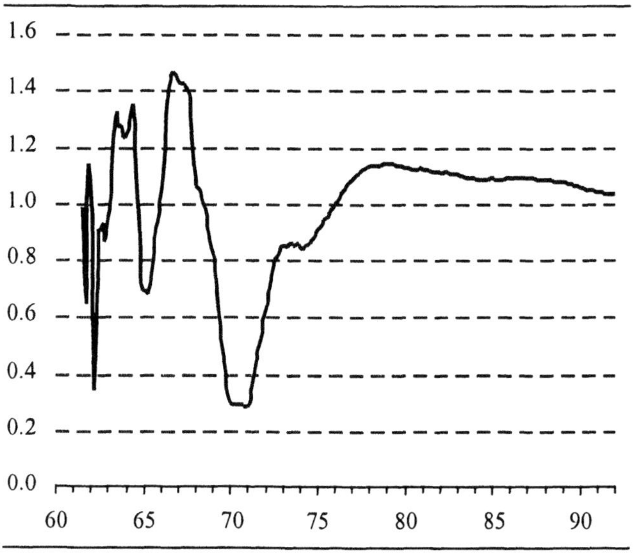

As a final measure to assess the validity of the restriction $\phi = 1$ estimates of ϕ in (11) are determined, expanding the estimation period by one observation at a time. These recursive estimates are shown in Figure 6.2. After rather erratic movements in the 1960s, the estimates have been nearly constant and approximately equal to 1 as from the end of the 1970s. From this additional analysis we conclude that imposing the restriction $\phi = 1$ in (11) is allowed and that the results in Table 6.1 are plausible. The empirical analysis conducted offers the opportunity to compare the price movements in The Netherlands and in Germany before and after the establishment of the EMS. In this way, the size of the reduction in the inflation rate associated with the reorientation in Dutch exchange rate policy can be determined. The estimation results reported in Table 1 show that the coefficient of the trend variable for the pre-EMS period is markedly higher for The Netherlands than for Germany. This reflects the higher inflation rate in The Netherlands, as shown before in Figure 6.1. From Table 6.1 it follows that the Dutch structural inflation rate during the pre-EMS period, defined as the slope of the deterministic part of the price process and calculated on an annual basis, is equal to 6.6%, whereas for Germany a figure of 4.2% results. During the EMS period, the structural inflation rate is equal 3.0% for both The Netherlands and Germany. The reduction in the Dutch inflation rate of 3.6 percentage points is therefore much larger than in Germany. This reduction is partly accounted for by the global downward trend in inflation in the 1980s. If this part is assumed equal to the inflation rate reduction found for Germany, the conclusion follows that an 2.4 percentage point decrease in the Dutch inflation rate can be ascribed to domestic factors such as the monetary and fiscal policies conducted and the behaviour of employers' organizations and trade unions. Under the assumption that the behaviour of government, employers and employees are the result disciplinating effects of the credible guilder-Dmark peg, it follows that two-thirds of the total inflation rate reduction can be attributed to the policy change, whereby the co-movement of Dutch and German inflation rates became to serve as the central objective.

6.4 Concluding remarks

This chapter investigates the long-run relationship between Dutch and German consumer prices during the period 1961-1991. Two questions are examined. The first deals with the ultimate objective of the guilder-Dmark peg, *viz.* whether the Dutch and German inflation rates move in line. The second question is whether Dutch and German prices are cointegrated. If this is the case, a price shock in The Netherlands is eventually adjusted, insofar as it deviates from that in Germany. If, in the long run, Dutch and German inflation rates are equal and the prices in both countries are cointegrated, Dutch competitiveness with respect to Germany - to the extent that it is reflected by the prices - remains constant. The empirical analysis shows that the answer to both questions is affirmative.

The empirical evidence indicates that the structural inflation in The Netherlands during the pre-EMS period 1961-1979 was 6.6%, whereas during the EMS period this rate was equal to 3.0%. For Germany, the respective percentages are 4.2% and 3.0%. Two-thirds of the reduction in the Dutch inflation rate can be attributed to the policy shift in 1979, implying that as a result of the guilder-Dmark peg, the objective has been that the Dutch inflation rate is in line with that in Germany.

Appendix to chapter 6

This Appendix discusses the results of the integration analysis, in which no allowance is made for possible structural changes. The order of integration is examined with the following model:

$$\Delta x_t = \rho\, x_{t-1} + \beta + \gamma\, tr_t + \varepsilon_t \qquad \text{(A)}$$

where x_t is the variable to be analysed. To eliminate residual autocorrelation, significant lags of Δx_t are included as additional explanatory variables in (A). To test the null hypothesis that x_t is integrated of order 1, we considered three statistics: $T\hat{\rho}$, where T is the number of observations, the t-ratio of $\hat{\rho}$ $\left(t(\hat{\rho})\right)$ and the F-statistic for the restriction $\rho = \gamma = 0 \left(F(\hat{\rho},\hat{\gamma})\right)$.

The procedure is applied to Dutch and German prices, as well as to the Dutch-German price ratio. Besides the entire sample period, we also examined the EMS period individually. The results are summarized in Table 6.2. For the EMS period two out of three statistics indicate trend-stationarity for the individual price series. However, the results obtained for the relative price ratio indicate difference-stationarity. The results obtained for the entire sample period 1961-1991 are mutually consistent. All statistics indicate that both the individual price variables and the relative price ratio are difference-stationary.

Table 6.2: Results of integration analysis

Variable	Estimation period	$T\hat{\rho}$	$t(\hat{\rho})$	$F(\hat{\rho},\hat{\gamma})$
Ln(Pnl)	61:1-91:12	-1.73	-1.45	1.98
	79:4-91:12	-3.36	-4.10*	8.42*
Ln(Pge)	61:1-91:12	-2.70	-2.62	3.46
	79:4-91:12	-3.36	-3.42*	6.31*
Ln(Pnl/Pge)	61:1-91:12	-0.91	-0.43	3.73
	79:4-91:12	-6.28	-1.80	1.61

Note: * indicates significance at a level of 0.05.

7 SUMMARY AND CONCLUDING REMARKS

7.1 Summary

Central in the conduct of monetary policy is the concept of monetary transmission, i.e. the processes that lie between adjusting instrument variables by the policy maker and the effects on the ultimate target variables. We start this book by stressing the complexity of the monetary transmission mechanism. Economic theory only provides some basic notions, and there exists considerable ambiguity regarding the various transmission channels actually operating in the economy, as well as their 'signs'. Given this uncertainty, we propose a general framework for preparing a strategy of monetary policy. Characteristic of our proposal is a multi-model approach, where the policy maker instead of using a single model designed to answer all questions uses a range of relatively small models, dealing with specific chains in the transmission mechanism. The choice of models is to be determined by the level of abstraction required by the problem at hand. The objective of this approach is to provide the policy maker with stable, economically interpretable relationships which can be used for policy purposes.

We illustrate this approach with five case studies, each dealing with different stages of the monetary transmission mechanism. The subjects of these studies fall into two categories: expectations and international interdependencies. As mentioned in the first chapter, both are important factors influencing the transmission mechanism. Notwithstanding this, they receive relatively little attention in empirical work on the subject. This provides the main motivation of our choice of subjects. The role of expectations is highlighted in chapters 2 and 5, in which the information content for monetary policy of, respectively, the yield curve and future inflation expected by consumers is discussed. The influence of international linkages is investigated with respect to three separate elements of the transmission mechanism: the long-term interest rate (chapter 3), real output (the business cycle, chapter 4) and the inflation rate (chapter 6).

In chapter two we study the relationship between the term structure of interest rates and non-financial activity: that is, real output and inflation. We argue that such a relationship can be interpreted as a (semi) reduced form of a dynamic macro-economic model where both long-term and short-term interest rates are jointly determined. Economic theory thus predicts a reduced-form like relationship between differences in observed interest rates on financial instruments with varying maturities on the one hand and unobservable differences in expected inflation rates and in expected real interest rates on the other hand. [1] The latter provide information on expected movements in future real output. The yield curve thus, in principle, incorporates information relevant for the monetary policy maker. We review the empirical evidence regarding the information content of the yield curve, and conclude that there exists considerable uncertainty in this respect. The evidence favouring the yield curve as leading indicator for inflation is not very convincing, because it is difficult to discriminate empirically between the effects on the curve of future real interest rates and of future inflation. On the other hand, the yield curve is a stable leading indicator for future real economic activity. There are, however, several interpretations of this relationship, depending on the nature of shocks hitting the economy and the speed of price adjustment. The latter, in turn, illustrates the importance of institutional factors as the functioning of credit, labour and product markets, as mentioned in the first chapter.

In chapter three we investigate the international co-movement of long-term interest rates, in terms of the standard (uncovered) interest parity relation stating that the difference between any two countries' nominal interest rates equals the expected depreciation of the first country's currency against the second's (over the life of the instrument), plus a risk premium. This parity relation functions as a benchmark to assess the degree of co-movement. Financial liberalisation and innovation, more specifically the development of the cross-currency interest rate swap market, increase the possibilities for hedging long-term currency positions. This could imply a stronger tendency towards co-movement of financial variables, such as bond yields. As a result, the uncovered interest rate parity relationship, the use of which was previously confined to short-term interest rates, can be applied to longer-term interest rates as well. This has consequences for the policy maker, as long-term interest rates in most countries are more relevant for the business cycle than short-term rates. Central to uncovered interest rate parity are (exchange rate) expectations, and in our empirical analysis we use survey data to measure them. Co-movement is analysed from a bilateral as well as from a multilateral perspective. Putting our reduced form to the test empirically, we find no evidence of an increased international interdependence in long-term interest rates. Although in line with most of the academic literature, this result is somewhat counterintuitive. Increased deregulation stimulates innovations on financial markets and increases the mobility of capital. This surely increases the opportunities for arbitrage and for an increase in the international interdependence of bond yields. However, our findings indicate that these opportunities remain to be realised. Possible explanations include the empirical rejection of the (sometimes stringent) assumptions used to

[1] In this overview, we neglect the role played by risk premia. See chapter 2 for a discussion.

construct the theoretical model from which the reduced form (uncovered interest rate parity) is derived. It could furthermore be the case that structural imbalances (for example on the budgetary front) in the countries investigated cause national factors to exert an important influence on bond yields, inhibiting increased interdependence.

In chapter four we develop leading indicators for fifteen industrialised countries, which enable us to forecast the business cycle fairly reliably between 4 to 6 months ahead. These leading indicators can be interpreted as reduced forms, relating various currently observed variables to the unobservable future business cycle. Given the non-neutrality of money in the short term (see chapter 1), these leading indicators are by themselves of interest for monetary policy makers as information variables. The measures of future economic activity in addition allow us to explore the international interdependence of business cycles, which, as mentioned earlier, is also relevant in the context of monetary transmission. In line with the findings of the previous chapter, the empirical analysis does not reveal any tendency towards increased international interdependencies between national business cycles over time. For some countries, however, especially in Europe, economic interdependence is already particularly strong. A result that is of interest with respect to our study of the role of expectations is that we find empirical support for the proposition that expectations of economic agents are important factors shaping the future business cycle: variables reflecting expectations of consumers and producers have a large predictive content concerning future output, albeit for relatively short horizons.

We explicitly deal with expectations in chapter five, when we assess the information content of the qualitative responses of consumers to surveys regarding perceived past and expected future price developments. A first task is to specify a theoretical framework that can be used to convert these qualitative survey responses into quantitative time series of expected inflation. Central to this conversion is the assumption that respondents answer the survey questions on the basis of probability distributions. Following an empirical analysis of the accuracy and other time series properties of the derived measures of expected inflation, we next investigate the relevance of these measures for monetary policy. This could be the case in, for example, the direct inflation targeting strategy, in which projections of inflation by the policy maker play a central role. We find that the derived inflation expectations are cointegrated with future inflation, thereby indicating their potential usefulness as information variables for monetary policy. However, since the expectations are not a causal determinant of future inflation, we conclude that caution is warranted in using these direct measures of inflation expectations for monetary policy purposes, even as information variables.

In chapter six the long-run relationship between Dutch and German consumer price levels is investigated. We derive an empirical relationship between Dutch and German consumer price levels which, *inter alia*, enables the policy maker to gauge whether the policy conducted, i.e. aiming at maintaining a stable exchange rate of the guilder *vis-à-vis* the Deutsche mark, has resulted in similar price movements in the two countries. We show that the ultimate objective of this peg, an inflation rate which is in line with the relatively low inflation rate in Germany, has indeed been realised. Moreover, Dutch and German price levels are found to be cointegrated. As a result, a price shock in the Netherlands is eventually adjusted, insofar as it deviates from that in Germany. With similar inflation rates in both countries, and price levels forming a cointegrating relationship, Dutch competitiveness with respect to Germany, to the extent that it is reflected in consumer prices, remains constant.

7.2 Concluding remarks

In line with the objective of our general framework, that is to provide the policy maker with stable, economically interpretable relationships which can be used for monetary policy purposes, we conclude by providing the policy maker with some of these relationships. These relationships are derived from the five cases studied.

1. Domestic economic fundamentals continue to be key factors shaping movements in long-term interest rates among the major industrialized countries, despite the international integration of financial markets. This means that the domestic policy maker still exerts considerable influence on domestic long-term interest rates, via the expectations of economic agents about future short-term interest rates. It also has implications for the supranational policy maker, as discussed in point 6 below.
2. The policy maker should be cautious in using the information contained in the yield curve for monetary policy purposes. The reduced form-like relationship which the yield curve depicts, is consistent with different underlying economic structures. Thus, different economic phenomena could lie behind the same observed movement in the yield spread, and the proper monetary policy response could, in principle, be different for these phenomena.
3. A similar conclusion applies to measures of expected inflation derived from consumer surveys. These measures provide information regarding future inflation, but are no causal determinants of inflation. Monetary policy wants to respond to underlying sources of inflationary pressure. Our direct measures of expectations do not qualify as such. The

usefulness of the latter hinges on the understanding of economic agents of the relationship between the underlying sources of inflation and inflation itself, and the fact that agents act upon that understanding. This understanding, however, could radically change in the case of a policy intervention that modifies the relationship between the underlying states and the inflation that eventually occurs.

4. Although the international linkages between national business cycles did not increase in the period 1975-1990, economic interdependence between the different countries in Europe is particularly strong. The single monetary policy which became operational in the euro area in January 1999 takes this into account, in that monetary policy makers now focus on economic conditions in the euro area as a whole, instead of individual countries.
5. The Dutch case study moreover illustrates that by recognising and using the economic interdependence, the need for an independent national monetary policy can be eliminated. The high interdependence of European economies, more specifically the real economic integration of the Dutch and German economies, was recognised by Dutch monetary authorities and exploited for policy purposes, by pegging the exchange rate of the Guilder to the D-mark. In doing so, they succeeded in bringing the Dutch inflation rate in line with the relatively low inflation rate in Germany, and keeping it there.
6. There is an implication for European Monetary Union that follows from our three case studies on economic interdependence. A prerequisite for a succesful monetary union, a sufficient degree of integration of real economic activity, seems to be satisfied for at least the core countries. This is indicated by the strong interdependence of the business cycles of these countries as well as by the success of Dutch monetary policy, which would not have been possible without such an integration. However, the lack of increasing interdependence of bond yields indicates that there remain some important national imbalances to correct, for example in the fiscal positions of the respective governments.

The five case studies illustrate that it is possible to simplify the interactions between various endogenous and policy instruments that take place in different chains of the monetary transmission mechanism. This simplification entails transforming some of the interactions into simple relationships, using different types of models to address different issues. Although this multi-model approach provides the policy maker with useful information regarding specific issues in the mechanism of monetary transmission, some of our studies, in particular those regarding the direct measures of expectations (i.e. those derived from survey data and from yield curves), illustrate the limitations of our approach. It is not always clear how the reduced-form like relationships pertaining to these expectational variables could serve as guidelines for the policy maker, as their interpretation is ambiguous. In that case, the information supplied by them will have to be conditioned by the understanding of the policy maker of the structural relationships between the variables incorporated in the various relationships. This understanding is also the key to the assessment by the policy maker of the weights to be given to the information coming from different models.

We conclude with two remarks. First, as mentioned in the introductionary chapter, we in our search for stable relationships make use of conventional statistical and econometric methods. These are conventional in the sense that they reduce all uncertainty to the probabilistic kind. Failing to find stable relationships using these methods however does not imply the actual absence of stability, as fundamental uncertainty (which rejects the frequency approach as a general theory of uncertainty) can give rise to stable behaviour which our methods by construction are unable to detect. Second, this study started with the hypothesis that, given the complexities and uncertainties inherent in the transmission mechanism, the role of structural econometric models in the preparation of monetary policy should be downplayed. Instead of using a single (large) structural model, the policy maker should use a range of different models, the selection of which is to be determined by the problem at hand. With the qualification that we illustrated this approach with only a limited number of case studies, the results of the previous chapters leave us with the impression that perhaps this hypothesis is in need of modification. Structural models are an indispensible ingredient in the preparation of monetary policy. It is the interaction of structural and other models that is likely to provide the largest gains in the preparation of monetary policy. A study of this interaction is, however, left as an important topic for future research.

References

Abel, A.B. (1996), 'Options, the value of capital, and investment', Quarterly Journal of Economics, 111, pp. 753-777.

Abuaf, N. and Jorion, P. (1990), 'Purchasing power parity in the long run', The Journal of Finance', 45, pp. 157-174.

Aizenman, J. and Frenkel, J.A. (1986), 'Targeting rules for monetary policy', Economics Letters, 21, pp. 183-187.

Akerlof, G., Dickens, W. and Perry, G. (1996), 'The macroeconomics of low inflation', Brookings Papers on Economic Activity, 1, pp. 1-59.

Andersen, O. (1952), 'The business test of the IFO-Institute for Economic Research, Munich, and its theoretical model', Review of the International Statistical Institute, 20, pp. 1-17.

Andersen, T.M. and J.R. Sørensen (1991), 'Uncertain exchange rate policies and interest rate determination', Kredit und Kapital, 31, pp. 468-483.

Asako, K. and Wagner, H. (1992), 'Nominal income targeting versus money supply targeting', Scottish Journal of Political Economy, 39, pp. 167-187.

Auerbach, A.J., 1982, 'The index of leading indicators: measurement without theory', thirty-five years later', Review of Economics and Statistics, 64, pp. 589-595.

Balcombe, K. (1996), 'The Carlson-Parkin method applied to NZ price expectations using QSBO survey data', Economics Letters, 51, pp. 51-57.

Ball, L. (1997), 'Efficient rules for monetary policy', NBER Working Paper, no 5952, Cambridge (MA).

Ball, L. and Mankiw, N.G. (1994), 'A sticky price manifesto', NBER Working Paper, no 4677, Cambridge (MA).

Ball,L., Mankiw, N.G. and Romer, D. (1988), 'The new Keynesian Economics and the output-inflation trade-off', Brookings Papers on Economic Activity, 1, pp. 1-65.

Bank of England (1990), 'The interest rate transmission mechanism in the United Kingdom and overseas', Quarterly Bulletin, 30, pp. 198-214.

Barrell, R. (1990), 'Has the EMS changed wage and price behaviour in Europe?', National Institute Economic Review, November, pp. 64-72.

Barro, R. (1995), 'Inflation and economic growth', Bank of England Quarterly Bulletin, 35, pp. 166-176.

Barro, R.J. and Gordon , D.B. (1983), 'A positive theory of monetary policy in a natural rate model', Journal of Political Economy, 91, pp. 589-610.

Basmann, R.L. (1972), 'The Brookings quarterly econometric model: science or number mysticism?', in Brunner, K. (ed), Problems and Issues in Current Econometric Practice, The Ohio State University, Columbus, Ohio, pp. 3-51.

Batchelor, R.A. (1981), 'Expectations, Output and Inflation: The european experience', European Economic Review, 17, pp. 1-25.

Batchelor, R.A. (1982), 'Aggregate expectations under the stable laws', Journal of Econometrics, 16, pp. 199-210.

Batchelor, R.A. (1986), 'Quantitative versus qualitative measures of inflation expectations', Oxford Bulletin of Economics and Statistics, 48, pp. 99-120.

Batchelor, R.A. and Dua, P. (1987), 'The accuracy and rationality of UK inflation expectations: some quantitative evidence', Applied Economics, 19, pp. 819-828.

Batchelor, R.A. and Dua, P. (1992), 'Survey expectations in the time series consumption function', The Review of Economics and Statistics, 74, pp. 598-606.

Baumgartner, J. , Ramaswamy, R. and Zettergren, G. (1997), 'Monetary policy and leading indicators of inflation in Sweden', IMF Working Paper no WP/97/34, IMF, Washington.

Beaufort Wijnholds, J.O. de, Eijffinger, S.C.W. and Hoogduin, L.H. (1994), 'A framework for monetary stability', Kluwer Academic Publishers, Dordrecht.

Berk, J.M. and Bikker, J.A. (1995), 'International Interdependence of Business Cycles in Manufacturing Industry: The Use of Leading Indicators for Forecasting and Analysis', Journal of Forecasting, 14, pp. 1-23.

Berk, J.M. and Bikker, J.A. (1994), 'The international business cycle and economic growth: analysis forecasting with leading indicators', Quarterly Bulletin nr 1, De Nederlandsche Bank, pp. 17-37.

Berk, J.M. and Winder, C.C.A. (1994), 'Price movements in the Netherlands and Germany and the guilder D-mark peg', De Economist, 142, pp. 63-74.

Berk, J.M. (1993), 'The present cyclical downturn in a historical perspective', Quarterly Bulletin nr 1, De Nederlandsche Bank, pp. 1-11.

Bernanke, B.S. (1993a), 'Credit in the macroeconomy', Federal Reserve Bank of New York Quarterly Review, 18, pp. 50-70.

Bernanke, B.S. (1993b), 'How important is the credit channel in the transmission of monetary policy? A comment', Carnegie-Rochester Conference Series on Public Policy, 39, pp. 47-52.

Bernanke, B.S. and Blinder, A.S. (1988), 'Credit, money, and aggregate demand', The American Economic Review, 78, pp. 435-439.

Bernanke, B.S. and Blinder, A.S. (1992), 'The Federal Funds Rate and the channels of monetary transmission', The American Economic Review, 82, pp. 901-921.

Bernanke, B.S. and Gertler, M. (1995), 'Inside the black box: The Credit Channel of monetary policy transmission', Journal of Economic Perspectives, 9, pp. 27-48.

Bernanke, B.S. and James, H. (1991), 'The gold standard, deflation and financial crisis in the Great Depression: an international comparison', in Hubbard, R.G. (ed), Financial Markets and Financial Crises, University of Chicago Press, Chicago, pp. 33-68.

Bernanke, B.S. and Mishkin, F.S. (1997), 'Inflation targeting: a new framework for monetary policy?', Journal of Economic Perspectives, 11, pp. 97-116.

Bernanke, B.S., Gertler, M. and Gilchrist, S. (1996), 'The financial accelerator and the flight to quality', The Review of Economics and Statistics, 78, pp. 1-15.

Bernanke,B.S. (1983), 'Nonmonetary effects of the financial crisis in the propagation of the great depression', The American Economic Review, 73, pp. 257-276.

Bernard, H. and Gerlach, S. (1996), 'Does the Term Structure predict Recessions? The International Evidence', BIS Working Paper no 37, BIS, Basle.

Beveridge, S., and C. Nelson (1981), 'A new approach to decomposition of economic time series into permanent and transitory components with particular attention to measurement of the 'business cycle'', Journal of Monetary Economics, 7, pp. 151-174.

Bikker, J.A. (1987), 'An international trade flow model with substitution: an extension of the gravity model', Kyklos, 40, pp. 315-337.

Bikker, J.A. (1993), 'Interdependence between the Netherlands and Germany: forecasting with VAR models, De Economist, 141, pp. 43-69.

Bikker, J.A., and L. de Haan (1988), Forecasting business cycles; a leading indicator for the Netherlands, Quarterly Bulletin nr 3, De Nederlandsche Bank, pp. 71-82.

Bikker, J.A., and L. de Haan (1990), 'DNB-conjunctuurindicator: een terugblik op vooruitzien (The DNB leading indicator: the art of looking ahead in retrospect)', ESB, pp. 1188-1192 (in Dutch).

BIS (1994), 'National differences in interest rate transmission', CB 393, BIS, Basle.

BIS (1995), 'Financial Structure and the monetary policy transmission mechanism', CB 394, BIS, Basle.

BIS (1996), 'The determinants of long-term interest rates and exchange rates and the role of expectations', conference papers, 2, BIS, Basle.

Blanchard , O.J. (1990), 'Why does money affect output? A survey', in Friedman, B.M. and Hahn, F.H. (eds), Handbook of Monetary Economics, vol 2, North-Holland, Amsterdam, 1990, pp. 779-835.

Blanchard, O.J. and Fischer, S. (1989), 'Lectures on macroeconomics', The MIT Press, Cambridge (MA).

Blanchard, O.J. and Summers, L.H. (1987), 'Hysteresis in unemployment', European Economic Review, 31, pp. 288-295.

Blinder, A.S. (1991), 'Why are prices sticky? Preliminary results from an interview study', The American Economic Review, (papers and proceedings), 81, pp. 89-96.

Blinder, A.S. (1994), 'On sticky prices: academic theories meet the real world', in Mankiw, N.G. (ed), 'Monetary Policy', University of Chicago Press, Chicago, pp. 117-154.

Blinder, A.S. (1997), 'What central bankers could learn from academics and vice versa', Journal of Economic Perspectives, 11, pp. 3-21.

Blundell-Wignall, A. and Browne, F. (1991), 'Increasing financial market integration, real exchange rates and macroeconomic adjustment', OECD Economics Department Working Paper, 96.

Bomhoff , E.J. (1994), 'Het Centraal Planbureau en lagere belastingen', Economisch-Statistische Berichten, 79, pp. 289-293 (in Dutch).

Boot, J.C.G., W. Feibes and J.H.C. Lisman (1967), 'Further methods of derivation of quarterly figures from annual data', Applied Statistics, 16, pp. 65-75.

Boschan, Ch., and W.W. Ebanks (1978), 'The phase-average trend: a new way of measuring economic growth', Proceedings of the business and economic statistics section, American Statistical Association, pp. 332-335.

Brandner, P., and K. Neusser (1992), 'Business cycles in open economies: stylized facts for Austria and Germany', Weltwirtschaftliches Archiv, 128, pp. 67-87.

Breeden, D.T. (1979), 'An Intertemporal Asset Pricing Model with Stochastic Consumption and Investment Opportunities', Journal of Financial Economics, 7, pp. 265-296.

Brennan, M.J. and Schwartz, E.S. (1979), 'A Continuous Time Approach to the Pricing of Bonds', Journal of Banking and Finance, 3, pp. 133-155.

Britton, E. and Whitley, J. (1997), 'Comparing the monetary transmission mechanism in France, Germany and the Unitee Kingdom', Bank of England Quarterly Bulletin, 37, pp. 152-162.

Brown, B.W. and Maital, S. (1981), 'What do economists know? An empirical study of experts' expectations', Econometrica, 49, pp. 491-504.

Browne, F. and Tease, W. (1992), 'The information content of interest rate spreads across financial systems', OECD Economics Department Working Paper, 109.

Brunner, K. (1971), 'A survey of selected issues in monetary theory', Swiss Journal of Economics and Statistics, 107, pp. 1-147.

Brunner, K. and Meltzer, A.H. (1976), 'An aggregative theory for a closed economy', in Stein, J. (ed), Monetarism, North-Holland, Amsterdam, 1976, pp. 69-103.

Bry, G. and Boschan, Ch. (1971), 'Cyclical analysis of time series: selected procedures and computer programs', Technical Paper 20 NBER, Columbia University Press.

Bryan, M.F. and Gavin, W.T. (1994), 'A different kind of money illusion: the case of long and variable lags', Journal of Policy Modeling, 16, pp. 529-540.

Bryant, R.C. (1983), 'Controlling money: The Federal Reserve and its critics', The Brookings Institution, Washington

Bryant, R.C. (1980), 'Money and monetary policy in interdependent nations', The Brookings Institution, Washington.

Bryant, R.C., Hooper, P. and Mann, C.L. (1993), 'Evaluating Policy Regimes: New Research in Empirical Macroeconomics', The Brookings Institution, Washington.

Buiter , W.H. (1988), 'Macroeconomic modelling for economic policy-comments', in Driehuis, W., Fase, M.M.G. and Den Hartog, H. (eds), Challenges for macroeconomic modelling, North-Holland, Amsterdam, 1988, pp. 137-145.

Bullard, J. and Keating, J.W. (1995), 'The long-run relationship between inflation and output in postwar economies', Journal of Monetary Economics, 36, pp. 477-496.

Burger, A.E. (1971), 'The money supply process', Wadsworth publishing company, WAAR??.

Burley, S.P. (1971), 'The principal component of the business cycle', International Economic Review, pp. 511-514.

Burns, A.F., and W.C. Mitchell (1938), 'Statistical indicators of cyclical revivals', Bulletin 69, NBER, Cambridge (Mass.).

Burns, A.F., and W.C. Mitchell (1946), 'Measuring business cycles', Studies in Business Cycles, 2, NBER, Cambridge (Mass.).

Butter, F.A.G. den, and M.M.G. Fase (1991), 'Seasonal Adjustment as a Practical Problem', Amsterdam: North-Holland, Amsterdam.

Butter, F.A.G. den, and T.J. Mourik (1990), 'Seasonal adjustment using structural time series models: an application and a comparison with the Census X-11 method', Journal of Business and Economic Statistics, 8, pp. 385-394.

Campbell, J.Y. and Perron, P. (1991), 'Pitfalls and opportunities: what macroeconomists should know about unit roots', in Blanchard, O.J. and Fisher, S. (eds), NBER Macroeconomics Annual 1991, pp. 141-219.

Campbell, J.Y. and Shiller, R.J. (1987), 'Cointegration and Tests of Present Value Models', Journal of Political Economy, 95, pp. 1062-1088.

Campbell, J.Y. and Shiller, R.J. (1991), 'Yield Spreads and Interest Rate Movements: A Bird's Eye View', Review of Economic Studies, 58, pp. 495-514.

Campbell, T.S., (1982), 'Financial Institutions, Markets and Economic Activity', McGraw-Hill, New York.

Canova, F. (1993), 'Detrending and business cycle facts', CEPR Discussion Papers, 782, CEPR, London.

Carlson, J.A. (1975), 'Are price expectations normally distributed?', Journal of the American Statistical Association, 70, pp. 749-754.

Carlson, J.A. and Parkin, M. (1977), 'Inflation expectations', Economica, 42, pp. 123-138.

Cavaglia, S. and Wolff, C.C.P. (1996), 'A note on the determinants of unexpected exchange rate movements', Journal of Banking and Finance, 20, pp. 179-188.

Cavaglia, S., Verschoor, W.F.C., and Wolff, C.C.P (1993), 'Further evidence on exchange rate expectations', Journal of International Money and Finance, 12, pp. 78-98.

Chan, K.C., Karolyi, G.A., Longstaff, F.A. and Sanders, A.B. (1992), 'An empirical comparison of alternative models of the short-term interest rate', Journal of Finance, 47, pp. 1209-1227.

Chan-Lee, J.H. (1980), 'A review of recent work in the area of inflationary expectations', Weltwirtschaftliches Archiv, 116, pp. 45-86.

Cherif, M., and V.A. Ginsburg (1976), 'Economic interdependence among the EEC countries: an unconventional view', European Economic Review, 8, pp. 71-85.

Cheung, Y.W. and Chinn, M.D. (1997), 'Integration, cointegration and the forecast consistency of structural exchange rate models', NBER Working Paper no 5943, NBER, Cambridge (MA).

Chinn, M. and Frankel, J. (1994), 'Patterns in exchange rate forecasts for twenty-five currencies', Journal of Money, Credit and Banking, 26, pp.759-770.

Christiano, L.J., Eichenbaum, M. and Evans, C.L. (1996), 'Sticky prices and limited participation models of money: a comparison', Working Paper no 5804, NBER, Cambridge (MA).

Christiansen, H. and Pigott, C. (1997), 'Long-term interest rates in globalised markets', OECD Economics Department Working Paper, 175.

Clark, P.K. (1987), 'The cyclical component of U.S. economic activity', Quarterly Journal of Economics, 102, pp. 797-814.

Clinton, K. (1994), 'The Term Structure of Interest Rates as a Leading Indicator of Economic Activity: A Technical Note', Bank of Canada Review, Winter 1994/1995, pp. 21-40.

Cooley, T.F. and Prescott, E.C. (1976), 'Estimation in the presence of stochastic parameter variation', Econometrica, 44, pp. 167-184.

Cox, J.C., Ingersoll, J.E. and Ross, S.A. (1981), 'A Re-Examination of Traditional Hypotheses about the Term Structure of Interest Rates', Journal of Finance, 36, pp. 769-799.

Cox, J.C., Ingersoll, J.E. and Ross, S.A. (1985a), 'An Intertemporal General Equilibrium Model of Asset Prices', Econometrica, 53, pp. 363-384.

Cox, J.C., Ingersoll, J.E. and Ross, S.A. (1985b), 'A Theory of the Term Structure of Interest Rates', Econometrica, 53, pp. 385-407.

CPB, 1992, 'FKSEC, a macro-ecometric model for the Netherlands' Leiden/Antwerp: Central Planning Bureau, Stenfert Kroese.

Cramer , J.S. (1988), 'A research agenda: panel discussion on macroeconomic models', in Driehuis, W., Fase, M.M.G. and Den Hartog, H. (eds), Challenges for macroeconomic modelling, North-Holland, Amsterdam, 1988, pp. 15-17.

Crockett , A.D. (1994), 'Rules versus discretion in monetary policy', in de Beaufort Wijnholds et al (1994), pp. 165-185.

Crockett, A.D. (1993), 'Monetary Policy Implications of Increased Capital Flows', in: Changing Capital Markets: Implications for Monetary Policy, Federal Reserve Bank of Kansas City, pp. 331-365.

Crockett, A.D. (1994), 'Rules versus Discretion in Monetary Policy', in: A Framework for Monetary Stability, J.O. de Beaufort Wijnholds, S.C.W. Eijffinger and L.H. Hoogduin (eds), Kluwer, Dordrecht, pp. 165-184.

Cross, R. (ed), (1988), 'Unemployment, hysteresis, and the natural rate of unemployment', Basil Blackwell, Oxford.

Cukierman, A. (1992), 'Central bank strategy, credibility, and independence: theory and evidence', The MIT Press, Cambridge (MA).

Dale, S. and Haldane, A. (1993), 'Bank behaviour and the monetary transmission mechanism', Bank of England Quarterly Bulletin, 33 (November), pp. 478-491.

Danthine, J.P., and M. Girardin (1989), 'Business cycles in Switzerland: a comparative study', European Economic Review, 33, pp. 31-50.

Davis, E.P. and Fagan, G. (1994), 'Are Financial Spreads Useful Indicators of Future Inflation and Output Growth in EU Countries?', Mimeo, EMI, Frankfurt.

Davis, E.P. and Henry, S.G.B. (1994), 'The Use of Financial Spreads as Indicator Variables', IMF Staff Papers, 41, pp. 517-525.

De Grauwe, P. (1994), 'The economics of monetary integration', Oxford University Press.

De Leeuw, F. and McKelvey, M.J. (1981), 'Price expectations of business firms', Brookings Papers on Economic Activity, 1, pp. 299-313.

De Menil, G. and Bhalla, S.S. (1975), 'Direct measurement of popular price expectations', American Economic Review, 65, pp. 169-180.

Deacon, M. and Derry, A. (1994), 'Estimating the Term Structure of Interest Rates', Working Paper no 24, Bank of England, London.

Debelle, G. (1997), 'Inflation targeting in practice', IMF Working Paper, no WP/97/35, IMF, Washington.

Debelle, G. and Fischer, S. (1994), 'How independent should a central bank be?', in Fuhrer, J.C. (ed), 'Goals, Guidelines and Constraints facing Monetary Policymakers', Federal Reserve Bank of Boston Conference Series no 38, pp. ......

Defris, L.V. and Williams, R.A. (1979), 'Quantitative versus qualitative measures of price expectations', Economics Letters, 2, pp. 169-173.

Dickey, D.A. and Pantula, S.G. (1987), 'Determining the order of differencing in autoregressive processes', Journal of Business and Economic Statistics, 5, pp. 455-461.

Dieckheuer, G. (1974), 'Theoretische Untersuchungen zur Wirkungsverzogerung der Geldpolitik', Zeitschrift für die gesamte Staatswissenschaft, 130, pp. 421-445 (in German).

Dixit, A.K. (1995), 'Irreversible investment with uncertainty and scale economies', Journal of Economic Dynamics and Control, 19, pp. 327-350.

Dixit, A.K. and Pindyck, R.S. (1994), 'Investment under uncertainty', Princeton University Press, Princeton.

Dornbusch, R. (1980), 'Open economy macroeconomics', Basic Books, New York.

Dothan, L.U. (1978), 'On the Term Structure of Interest Rates', Journal of Financial Economics', 6, pp. 59-69.

Dréze, J. and Bean, C. (1990), 'European unemployment: lessons from a multicountry econometric study', Scandinavian Journal of Economics, 92, pp. 135-165.

Egebo, T. and Englander, A.S. (1992), 'Institutional commitments and policy credibility: a critical survey and empirical evidence from the ERM', OECD Economic Studies, 18.

Englander, A. and Stone, G. (1989), Inflation expectations surveys as predictors of inflation and behaviour in financial and labor markets', Research Paper no 8918, Federal Reserve Bank of New York, New York.

Engle, R.F. and Granger, C.W.J. (1987), 'Co-integration and error correction: representation, estimation and testing', Econometrica, 55, pp. 251-276.

Engle, R.F. and Granger, C.W.J. (1991), 'Long-run economic relationships: Readings in cointegration', Oxford University Press, Oxford.

Estrella, A. and Mishkin, F.S. (1996), 'Is there a role for monetary aggregates in the conduct of monetary policy?', NBER Working Paper, no 5845, Cambridge (MA).

Estrella, A. and Hardouvelis, G.A. (1991), 'The Term Structure as a Predictor of Real Economic Activity', The Journal of Finance, XLVI, pp. 555-576.

Estrella, A. and Mishkin, S. (1995), 'The Term Structure of Interest Rates and its Role in Monetary Policy for the European Central Bank', Research Paper no 9526, Federal Reserve Bank of New York, New York.

Estrella, A. and Mishkin, S. (1996), 'Predicting US Recessions: Financial Variables as Leading Indicators', Research Paper no 9609, Federal Reserve Bank of New York, New York.

European Communities, Commission of the (1982), 'The economic sentiment indicator: composition and method of calculation', European Economy, Suppl. B, 11.

European Monetary Institute (1997), 'The single monetary policy in stage three: elements of the monetary policy strategy of the ESCB', EMI, Frankfurt am Main.

Evans, G. and Gulamani, R. (1984), 'Tests for rationality of the Carlson-Parkin inflation expectations data', Oxford Bulletin of Economics and Statistics, 46, pp. 1-19.

Fair, R. (1996), 'Testing the standard view of the long-run unemployment-inflation relationship', Cowles Foundation Discussion Paper, 1121, Yale University.

Fama, E.F. (1990), 'Term-Structure Forecasts of Interest Rates, Inflation and Real Returns', Journal of Monetary Economics, 25, pp. 59-76.

Fama, E.G. and Bliss, R.R. (1987), 'The Information in Long-Maturity Forward Rates', American Economic Review, 77, pp. 680-692.

Fase, M.M.G. (1997), 'De risicopremie op aandelen in de Europese Unie', Onderzoeksrapport WOE no 487, De Nederlandsche Bank, Amsterdam.

Fase, M.M.G. and Vlaar, P.J.G. (1998), 'International convergence of capital market interest rates', De Economist, 146, pp. 257-269.

Fase, M.M.G. and Winder, C.C.H (1993), 'The Demand for Money in the Netherlands and the other EC Countries', De Economist, 141, pp. 471-496.

Fase, M.M.G. (1991), 'Forecasting is an art, even for the central bank', Quarterly Bulletin no 4, De Nederlandsche Bank, pp. 73-81.

Fase, M.M.G., and H.C.J. van der Wielen (1989), 'Grandeur en malheur van de conjunctuurbarometer' (The strengths and weaknesses of economic barometers), ESB, pp. 332-336 (in Dutch).

Fase, M.M.G., and J.A. Bikker (1985), 'De datering van economische fluctuaties: proeve van een conjunctuurspiegel voor Nederland 1965-1984' (The dating of economic fluctuations: testing a business cycle indicator for the Netherlands), Maandschrift Economie, pp. 229-332 (in Dutch).

Fase, M.M.G., Kramer, P. and Boeschoten, W.C. (1990), Morkmon II: het DNB kwartaalmodel voor Nederland', Monetaire Monografieën, 11, De Nederlandsche Bank, Amsterdam (in Dutch).

Federal Reserve Bank of Kansas City (1993), ' Changing capital markets: implications for monetary policy', Kansas City.

Feldstein, M. (1996), 'The costs and benefits of going from low inflation to price stability', NBER Working Paper, no 5469, Cambridge (MA).

Feldstein, M. and Stock, J.H. (1994), 'The use of a monetary aggregate to target nominal GDP', in Mankiw, N.G. (ed), 'Monetary Policy', University of Chicago Press, Chicago, pp. 7-69.

Fell, J.P.C. (1996), 'The role of short rates and foreign long rates in the determination of long-term interest rates, EMI Staff Paper, 4.

Figlewski, S. and Wachtel, P. (1981), 'The formation of inflationary expectations', The Review of Economics and Statistics, 63, pp. 1-10.

Fischer, A. M. (1989), 'Unit roots and survey data', Oxford Bulletin of Economics and Statistics, 51, pp. 451-463.

Fischer, S. (1996), 'Why are central banks pursuing long-run price stability?', in Federal Reserve Bank of Kansas City, 'Achieving Price Stability', Kansas City, pp. 7-35.

Fischer, S. (1977), 'Long-term contracts, rational expectations, and the optimal money supply rule', Journal of Political Economy, 85, pp. 191-206.

Fischer, S. (1981), 'Towards an understanding of the costs of inflation: II', in Brunner, K. and Meltzer, A.H. (eds), 'The costs and consequences of inflation', Carnegie-Rochester Conference Series on Public Policy, 15, 1981, pp. 5-42.

Fischer, S. (1994), 'Modern central banking', in Capie, F., Goodhart, C., Fischer, S. and Schnadt, N. (eds), 'The future of central banking. The Tercentenary Symposium of the Bank of England', The Cambridge University Press, Cambridge, pp. 262-308.

Fischer, S. and Modigliani, F. (1978), 'Towards an understanding of the real effects and costs of inflation', Weltwirtchaftliches Archiv, 114, pp. 810-832.

Fishe, R.P.H. and Lahiri, K. (1981), 'On the estimation of inflationary expectations from qualitative responses', Journal of Econometrics, 16, pp. 89-102.

Fisher, I. (1933), 'The debt-deflation theory of great depressions', Econometrica, 1, pp. 337-357.

Fletcher, D.J. and Taylor, L.W. (1996), 'Swap covered interest parity in long-date capital markets', Review of Economics and Statistics, 78, pp. 530-538.

Foley, D. and Sidrauski, M. (1971), 'Monetary and fiscal policy in a growing economy', MacMillan Series in Economics, Macmillan: London.

Foster, J. and Gregory, M. (1977), 'Inflation expectations: the use of qualitative survey data', Applied Economics, 9, pp. 319-329.

Frank, J. (1986), 'The New Keynesian Economics', Wheatsheaf Books, Brighton.

Frankel, J.A. (1989), 'International financial integration, relations among interest rates and exchange rates, and monetary indicators', in C. Pigott (ed.), International Financial Integration and US Monetary Policy, Federal Reserve Bank of New York.

Frankel, J.A. and Chinn, M. (1991), 'The stabilizing properties of a nominal GNP rule in an open economy', Working Paper, no 91-166, University of California at Berkeley.

Frankel, J.A. and Froot, K.A (1987), 'Using survey data to test standard propositions regarding exchange rate expectations', American Economic Review, 77, 133-153.

Freedman, C. (1996), 'What operating procedures should be adopted to maintain price stability-practical issues', in Federal Reserve Bank of Kansas City, 'Achieving Price Stability', pp. 241-287.

Friedman, B, M. (1993), 'The Role of Judgement and Discretion in the Conduct of Monetary Policy: Consequences of Changing Financial Markets', in: Changing Capital Markets: Implications for Monetary Policy, Federal Reserve Bank of Kansas City, pp. 151-197.

Friedman, B.M. (1975), 'Targets, instruments, and indicators of monetary policy', Journal of Monetary Economics, 1, pp. 443-473.

Friedman, B.M. (1977), 'The inefficiency of short-run monetary targets for monetary policy', Brookings Papers on Economic Activity, 2, pp. 293-335.

Friedman, B.M. (1983), 'The roles of money and credit in macroeconomic analysis', in Tobin, J. (ed), 'Macroeconomics, prices and quantities: Essays in honour of Arthur M. Okun', The Brookings Institution, Washington, pp. 161-189.

Friedman, B.M. (1990), 'Targets and instruments of monetary policy' , in Friedman, B.M. and Hahn, F.H. (eds), Handbook of Monetary Economics, vol 2, North-Holland, Amsterdam, pp. 1185-1230.

Friedman, B.M. (1993), 'The role of judgement and discretion in the conduct of monetary policy: consequences of changing financial markets', in Federal Reserve Bank of Kansas City (1993), 'Changing capital markets: implications for monetary policy', pp. 151-197.

Friedman, B.M. (1994), 'Intermediate Targets versus Information Variables as Operating Guides for Monetary Policy', in A Framework for Monetary Stability, J.O. de Beaufort Wijnholds, S.C.W. Eijffinger and L.H. Hoogduin (eds), Kluwer, Dordrecht, pp. 109-135.

Friedman, B.M. (1996), 'The rise and fall of money growth targets as guidelines for US monetary policy', NBER Working Paper, no 5465, Cambridge (MA).

Friedman, B.M. and Kuttner, K.N. (1992), 'Money, Income, Prices and Interest Rates', American Economic Review, 82, pp. 472-492.

Friedman, B.M. and Kuttner, K.N. (1993), 'Why does the paper-bill spread predict real economic activity?', in Stock, J.H. and Watson, M.W. (eds), 'Business Cycles, Indicators, and Forecasting', University of Chicago Press, Chicago, pp. 213-253.

Friedman, B.M. and Kuttner, K.N. (1996), 'A Price Target for US Monetary Policy? Lessons from the Experience with Money Growth Targets', Brookings Papers on Economic Activity, 1: 1996, pp. 77-146.

Friedman, M. (1959), 'The demand for money: some theoretical and empirical results', Journal of Political Economy, 67, pp. 327-351.

Friedman, M. (1961), 'The lag in the effect of monetary policy', Journal of Political Economy, 69, pp. 447-466.

Friedman, M. (1968), 'The role of monetary policy', The American Economic Review, 58, pp. 1-17.

Friedman, M. (1969), 'The optimum quantity of money and other essays', Aldine Publishing Company, Chicago.

Friedman, M. (1970), 'A theoretical framework for monetary analysis', Journal of Political Economy, 78, pp. 193-238. We used the version reprinted in Gordon (1974).

Friedman, M. (1982), 'Monetary policy: theory and practice', Journal of Money, Credit, and Banking, 14, pp. 98-118.

Friedman, M. and Schwartz, A. (1963), 'Money and Business Cycles', Review of Economics and Statistics, 45, reprinted in Friedman, M. (1969), pp. 189-237.

Froot, K.A. (1990), 'Short rates and expected asset returns', NBER Working Paper 3247.

Froot, K.A. and Frankel, J.A. (1989), 'Forward discount bias: Is it an exchange risk premium?', Quarterly Journal of Economics, 41, pp. 139-161.

Fuhrer, J.C. (1997), 'Central bank independence and inflation targeting: monetary policy paradigms for the next millennium?', New England Economic Review, Jan/Feb,Federal Reserve Bank of Boston, pp. 19-36.

Fuhrmann, W. (1980), 'Faktoranalytische Deskription des Konjunktur verbundes Zwischen der Bundesrepublik Deutschland, Schweden und den USA' (A factor-analytical description of the economic interdependence of Germany, Sweden and the USA), Jahrbuch fur National für konomie und Statistik, 195, pp. 303-321 (in German).

Fuller, W.A. (1976), 'Introduction to statistical time series', John Wiley and sons, New York.

Gagnon, J. E. and Unferth, M.D. (1995), 'Is there a world interest rate?', Journal of International Money and Finance, 14, pp. 845-855.

Garcia-Ferrer, A., and J. Del Hoyo (1992a), 'On trend extraction models: interpretation, empirical evidence and forecasting performance', Journal of Forecasting, 11, pp. 645-665.

Garcia-Ferrer, A., and J. Del Hoyo (1992b), 'On trend extraction models: reply on comments by Harvey', Journal of Forecasting, 11, pp. 673-674.

Garretsen, H. and Swank, J. (1997), 'The transmission of interest rate changes and the role of bank balance sheets: a VAR-analysis for the Netherlands', Journal of Macroeconomics, 20, pp. 325-339.

Gerlach, H.M.S. (1988), 'World business cycle under fixed and flexible exchange rates', Journal of Money, Credit and Banking, 20, pp. 621-632.

Gerlach, S. (1995), 'The Information Content of the Term Structure: Evidence for Germany', BIS Working Paper no 29, BIS, Basle.

Gerlach, S. (1996), 'Monetary Policy and the Behaviour of Interest Rates: Are Long Rates Excessively Volatile?', BIS Working Paper no 34, BIS, Basle.

Gerlach, S. and Smets, F. (1995), 'The Term Structure of Euro-Rates: Some Evidence in Support of the Expectations Hypothesis', BIS Working Paper no 28, BIS, Basle.

Ginsburg, V.A. (1973), 'The common market economics: interdependence or independence', European Economic Review, 4, pp. 289-291.

Goodhart, C.A.E and Viñals, J. (1994), 'Strategy and tactics of monetary policy: examples from Europe and the Antipodes', in Fuhrer, J.C. (ed), 'Goals, Guidelines and Constraints facing Monetary Policymakers', Federal Reserve Bank of Boston Conference Series no 38, pp. 139-194.

Gordon, R.J. (ed.) (1974), 'Milton Friedman's monetary framework: A debate with his critics', The University of Chicago Press, Chicago.

Gordon,R.J. (1990), 'What is New-Keynesian economics?', Journal of Economic Literature, 27, pp. 1115-1171.

Granger, C.W.J. and Newbold, P. (1973), 'Some comments on the evaluation of economic forecasts', Applied Economics, 5, pp. 35-47.

Granger, C.W.J. and Newbold, P. (1986), 'Forecasting economic time series', Academic Press, Orlando.

Granger, C.W.J. (1980), 'Forecasting in Business and Economics', Academic Press, New York.

Green, J.H. (1996), 'Inflation targeting: theory and policy implications', IMF Staff Papers, 43, pp. 779-795.

Groeneveld, J.M., Knot, K.H.W. and Wesseling, A.A.T. (1996), 'De monetaire beleidsstrategie van de ECB', Economisch-Statistische Berichten, 81, pp. 618-621 (in Dutch).

Hall, R.E. (1986), 'Market structure and macroeconomic fluctuations', Brookings Papers on Economic Activity, pp. 285-338.

Hall, S.G. and Henry, S.G.B. (1988), 'Macroeconomic modelling', North-Holland, Amsterdam.

Hamilton, J.D. (1994), 'Time series analysis', Princeton University Press, Princeton.

Hansen, L.P. (1982), 'Large sample properties of generalized method of moments estimators', Econometrica, 50, pp. 1029-1054.

Hansen, L.P. and Hodrick, R.J. (1980), 'Forward exchange rates as optimal predictors of future spot rates: an econometric analysis', Journal of Political Economy, 88, pp. 829-853.

Hardouvelis, G.A. (1988), 'The Predictive Power of the Term Structure during Recent Monetary Regimes', The Journal of Finance, 43, pp. 339-356.

Hardouvelis, G.A. (1994), 'The Term Structure Spread and Future Changes in Long and Short Rates in the G7 Countries', Journal of Monetary Economics, 33, pp. 255-283.

Harrod, R.F. (1939), 'An essay in dynamic theory', The Economic Journal, 49, pp........

Harvey, A.C. (1985),'Trends and cycles in macroeconomic time series', Journal of Business and Economic Statistics, 3, pp. 216-227.

Harvey, A.C. (1992), 'On trend extraction models: comments on a paper by Garcia-Ferrer and Del Hoyo', Journal of Forecasting, 11, pp. 669-672.

Harvey, A.C. (1993), Time Series Models, Harvester Wheatsheaf, New York.

Harvey, C.R. (1988), 'The Real Term Structure and Consumption Growth', Journal of Financial Economics, 22, pp. 305-333.

Harvey, C.R. (1991), 'Interest Rate Based Forecasts of German Economic Growth', Weltwirtschaftliches Archiv, 127, pp. 701-719.

Haubrich, J.G. and Dombrosky, A.M. (1996), 'Predicting Real Growth Using the Yield Curve', Economic Review 1996-I, Federal Reserve Bank of Cleveland, 32, pp. 26-35.

Heiner, R.A. (1983), 'The origin of predictable behaviour', American Economic Review, 73, pp. 560-595.

Henderson, D.W. and McKibbin, W.J. (1993), 'An assessment of some basic monetary policy regime pairs: analytical and simulation results from simple multiregion macroeconomic models', in Bryant et.al. (1993), pp. 45-218.

Hicks, J.R. (1974), 'The crisis in Keynesian economics', Basil Blackwell, Oxford.

Holden, K. and Peel, D.A. (1977), 'An empirical investigation of inflationary expectations', Oxford Bulletin of Economics and Statistics, 39, pp. 291-299.

Holden, K., Peel, D.A. and Thompson, J.L. (1990), 'Economic forecasting: an introduction', Cambridge University Press, Cambridge.

Holmes, M.J. and Wu, Y. (1997), 'Capital controls and covered interest rate parity in the EU: evidence from a panel-data unit root test', Weltwirtschaftliches Archiv, 133, pp. 76-89.

Hoogduin, L.H. (1991), 'Some aspects of uncertainty and the theory of a monetary economy', unpublished Phd-thesis, Groningen University.

Howe, H. and Pigott, C. (1991), 'Determinants of long-term interst rates: an empirical study of several industrial countries', Federal Reserve Bank of New York Quarterly Review, 16, pp. 12-28.

Howrey, E.P. (1969), 'Distributed lags and the effectiveness of monetary policy', The American Economic Review, 59, pp. 997-1001.

Hu, Z. (1993), 'The Yield Curve and Real Activity', IMF Staff Papers, 40, pp. 781-806.

Huang, B.N. and Yang, C.W. (1996), 'Long-run purchasing power parity revisited: a Monte Carlo simulation', Applied Economics, 28, pp. 967-974.

Hubbard, R.G. (1994a), 'Money, the financial system, and the economy', Addison-Westley Publishing Company, Reading (MA).

Hubbard, R.G. (1994b), 'Is there a credit channel for monetary policy?', NBER Working Paper, no 4977, Cambridge (MA).

Johansen, S. (1995), 'Likelihood-based inference in cointegrated vector autoregressive models', Oxford University Press, Oxford.

Johnson, N.L. and Kotz, S. (1970), 'Continuous univariate distributions, vols 1 and 2', John Wiley and Sons, New York.

Jondeau, E. and Ricart, R. (1996), 'The Expectations Theory: Tests on French, German, and American Euro-Rates', Notes D'Etudes et de Recherche no 35, Banque de France, Paris.

Jorion, P. and Mishkin, F.S. (1991), 'A Multicountry Comparison of Term Structure Forecasts at Long Horizons', Journal of Financial Economics, 29, pp. 59-80.

Juster, F.T. and Taylor, L.D. (1975), 'Towards a theory of saving behaviour', American Economic Review, Papers and Proceedings, 65, pp. 203-209.

Kahn, G.A. (1996), 'Symposium summary', in Federal Reserve Bank of Kansas City, 'Achieving Price Stability', pp.ix-xix.

Kareken, J.H., Muench, T. and Wallace, N. (1973), 'Optimal open market strategy: the use of information variables', The American Economic Review, 63, pp. pp.156-172.

Kashyap, A.K. and Stein, J.C. (1994), 'Monetary policy and bank lending', in Mankiw, N.G. (ed), 'Monetary Policy', University of Chicago Press, Chicago, pp. 221-256.

Kashyap, A.K., Stein, J.C. and Wilcox, D.W. (1993), 'Monetary Policy and credit conditions: evidence from the composition of external finance', The American Economic Review, 83, pp. 78-99.

Kasman, B. and Pigott, C. (1988), 'Interest rate divergences among the major industrial nations', Federal Reserve Bank of New York Quarterly Review, 13, pp. 28-44.

Kendall, M. and Stuart, A. (1977), 'The Advanced Theory of Statistics, Vol. I', Griffin & Co, London.

Kendall, M., and J.K. Ord, 1990, Time Series, Edward Arnold, Kent.

Keynes, J.M. (1936), 'The general theory of employment, interest and money', MacMillan, London.

King, M. (1996), 'How should central banks reduce inflation-conceptual issues', in Federal Reserve Bank of Kansas City, 'Achieving Price Stability', pp. 53-93..

Klein, P.A., and G.H. Moore (1983), 'The leading indicator approach to economic forecasting: retrospect and prospect', Journal of Forecasting 2, pp. 119-135.

Klein, P.A., and G.H. Moore (1985), 'Monitoring growth cycles in marketoriented countries: developing and using international economic indicators', NBER Studies in Business Cycles series no. 26, Cambridge (Mass.).

Kloek, T. (1988), 'Macroeconomic models and econometrics', in Driehuis, W., Fase, M.M.G. and Den Hartog, H. (eds), Challenges for macroeconomic modelling, North-Holland, Amsterdam, 1988, pp. 343-388.

Kloek, T., and R. Bannink (1962), 'Principal-component analysis applied to business test data', Statistica Neerlandica, 16, pp. 57-69.

Knöbl, A. (1974), 'Price expectations and actual price behaviour in Germany', IMF Staff Papers, 21, pp. 83-100.

Knot, K. (1996), 'Fiscal policy and interest rates in the European Union', Edward Elgar, Cheltenham.

Knot, K.H.W. and J. De Haan (1995), 'Interest differentials and exchange rate policies in Austria, the Netherlands, and Belgium', Journal of Banking and Finance, 19, pp. 363-386.

Koedijk, K.G. and Kool, C.J.M. (1995), 'Future Inflation and the Information in International Term Structures', Empirical Economics, 20, pp. 217-242.

Koopmans, T. (1947), 'Measurement without theory', Review of Economics and Statistics, 29, pp. 161-172.

Koutsoyiannis, A. (1977), 'Theory of Econometrics', Macmillan, London.

Kuipers, S.K. (1983), 'Macro-economische modelbouw in discussie V; Econometrische modellen: een onmisbaar hulpmiddel' , Economisch-Statistische Berichten, 68, pp.1140-1143 (in Dutch).

Kuismanen, M. and Spolander, M. (1994), 'Measuring inflation expectations in Finland: a survey data approach', Bank of Finland Discussion Papers no 21/94, Bank of Finland, Helsinki.

Kwiatkowski, D., Phillips, P.C.B., Schmidt, P. and Shin, Y. (1992), 'Testing the null hypothesis of stationarity against the alternative of a unit root', Journal of Econometrics, 54, pp. 159-178.

Kydland, F. and Prescott, E. (1977), 'Rules rather than discretion: the inconsistency of optimal plans', Journal of Political Economy, 85, pp. 473-492.

Lahiri, K., and G.H. Moore (1991), 'Leading Economic Indicators: New Approaches and Forecasting Record', Cambridge University Press.

Layard, R., Nickell, S. and Jackman, R. (1991), 'Unemployment. Macroeconomic performance and the labour market', Oxford University Press, Oxford.

Lecq, S.G. van der (1996), 'Conventions and institutions in coordination problems', De Economist, 144, pp. 397-428.

Leeper, E.M., Sims, C.A. and Zha, T. (1996), 'What does monetary policy do?', Brookings Papers on Economic Activity, 2, pp. 1-78.

Lindbeck, A. and Snower, D.J. (1987), 'Theories of Involuntary Unemployment. Efficiency Wages versus Insiders and Outsiders', European Economic Review, 31, pp. 407-416.

Loo, P.D. van (1984), 'De hoogte van de kapitaalmarktrente', Maandschrift Economie, 48, pp.123-139 (in Dutch).

Lucas, R.E, (1976),'Understanding business cycles', reprinted in Lucas, R.E. (1985), 'Studies in business cycle theory', The MIT Press, Cambridge (MA), pp. 215-239.

Lucas, R.E. (1972a), 'Expectations and the neutrality of money', Journal of Economic Theory, 4, pp. 103-124.

Lucas, R.E. (1972b), 'Econometric testing of the natural rate hypothesis', reprinted in Lucas, R.E. (1985), 'Studies in business cycle theory', The MIT Press, Cambridge (MA), pp. 90-104.

Lucas, R.E. (1973), 'Some international evidence on output-inflation tradeoffs', reprinted in Lucas, R.E. (1985), 'Studies in business cycle theory', The MIT Press, Cambridge (MA), pp. 131-145.

Lucas, R.E. (1976), 'Econometric policy evaluation: A critique', reprinted in Lucas, R.E. (1985), 'Studies in business cycle theory', The MIT Press, Cambridge (MA), pp. 104-131.

Lucas, R.E. (1977), 'Understanding business cycles', reprinted in Lucas, R.E. (1985), 'Studies in business cycle theory', The MIT Press, Cambridge (MA), pp. 215-240.

Lucas, R.E. (1978), 'Asset Prices in an Exchange Economy', Econometrica, 46, pp. 1429-1445.

Madsen, J.B. (1996), 'Formation of inflation expectations: from the simple to the rational expectations hypothesis', Applied Economics, 28, pp. 1331-1337.

Mankiw, N.G. and Romer, D. (1991), 'New Keynesian Economics', The MIT Press, Cambridge (MA).

Mauskopf, E. (1990), 'The transmission channels of monetary policy: how have they changed?', Federal Reserve Bulletin, 76, pp. 985-1008.

McAleer, M. and McKenzie, C.R. (1992), 'Recursive estimation and generated regressors', Economics Letters, 39, pp. 1-5.

McCallum , B.T. (1990), 'Targets, indicators and instruments of monetary policy', in Haraf, W.S. and Cagan, P. (eds), 'Monetary policy for a changing financial environment', American Enterprise Institute, Washington, pp. 44-70.

McCallum, B.T. (1985), 'On consequences and criticisms of monetary targeting', Journal of Money, Credit, and Banking, 17, pp. 570-597.

McCallum, B.T. (1994), 'A reconsideration of the uncovered interest parity relationship', Journal of Monetary Economics, 33, pp. 105-132.

McCallum, B.T. (1994), 'Monetary policy and the term structure of interest rates', Working Paper no 4938, NBER, Cambridge (MA).

Menon, J. (1995), 'Exchange rate passthrough', Journal of Economic Surveys, 9, pp. 197-231.

Merton, R.C. (1973), 'An Intertemporal Capital Asset Pricing Model', Econometrica, 41, pp. 867-887.

Mishkin, F.S. (1990a), 'The Information in the Longer Maturity Term Structure about Future Inflation', Quarterly Journal of Economics, 105, pp. 815-828.

Mishkin, F.S. (1990b), 'What Does the Term Structure Tell Us About Future Inflation?', Journal of Monetary Economics, 25, pp. 77-95.

Mishkin, F.S. (1991), 'Asymmetric information and financial crises: a historical perpsective', in Hubbard, R.G. (ed), Financial Markets and Financial Crises, University of Chicago Press, Chicago, pp.69-108.

Mishkin, F.S. (1991), 'A Multi-Country Study of the Information in the Shorter Maturity Term Structure about Future Inflation', Journal of International Money and Finance, 10, pp. 2-22.

Mishkin, F.S. (1995), 'Symposium on the monetary transmission mechanism', Journal of Economic Perspectives, 9, pp. 3-10.

Mishkin, F.S. (1996), 'The channels of transmission: lessons for monetary policy', NBER Working Paper, no 5464, Cambridge (MA).

Modigliani, F. and Miller, M.H. (1958), 'The cost of capital, corporation finance and the theory of investment', The American Economic Review, 48, pp. 261-297.

Modigliani, F. and Shiller, R. (1973), 'Inflation, rational expectations and the term structure of interest rates', Economica, 40, pp. 12-43.

Modigliani, F. and Sutch, R. (1966), 'Innovations in Interest Rate Policy', American Economic Review, 56, pp.178-197.

Moersch, M. (1996), 'Interest Rates or Spreads as Predictors of Real Economic Activity?', Konjunkturpolitik, 42, pp. 40-52.

Moore, G.H. (1961), Business Cycle Indicators, Contributions to the Analysis of Current Business Conditions, NBER, Princeton University Press.

Moore, G.H. (1975), 'The analysis of economic indicators', Scientific American, pp. 17-23.

Muth, J.F. (1961), 'Rational expectations and the theory of price movements', reprinted in Lucas, R.E. and Sargent, T.J. (eds), 'Rational expectations and econometric practice', George Allen and Unwin, London, pp. 3-23.

Nelson, C.R. (1972), 'The prediction performance of the FRB-MIT-PENN model of the US economy', American Economic Review, 62, pp. 902-917.

Nelson, C.R. and C.I. Plosser (1982), 'Trends and Random Walks in Macroeconomic Time Series - Some Evidence and Implications', Journal of Monetary Economics, 10, pp. 139-162

Newey, W.K. and West, K.D. (1987), 'A simple, positive semi-definite, heteroskedastisticity and autocorrelation consistent covariance matrix', Econometrica, 55, pp. 703-708.

Ng, C.N., and P.C. Young (1990), 'Recursive estimation and forecasting of non-stationary time series', Journal of Forecasting, 9, pp. 173-204.

OECD (1987), 'OECD Leading indicators and business cycles in member countries 1960-1985', Sources and Methods, 39, Paris.

OECD (1992), 'Comparison of the current downturn with past cyclical episodes', Economic Outlook, 52, pp. 31-40.

Okina, K. (1995), 'The policy objectives and the optimal institutional framework of a central bank', paper prepared for the conference 'Towards more effective monetary policy', Bank of Japan, October 1995.

Oliner, S.D. and Rudebusch, G.D. (1996), 'Is there a broad credit channel for monetary policy?', Federal Reserve Bank of San Fransisco Economic Review,1, pp. 3-13.

Öller, L.E. (1990), 'Forecasting the business cycle using survey data', International Journal of Forecasting, 6, pp. 453-461.

Pagan, A. (1984), 'Econometric issues in the analysis of regressions with generated regressors', International Economic Review, 25, pp. 221-247.

Palm, F.C. (1988), 'Macroeconomic models and econometrics-a comment', in Driehuis, W., Fase, M.M.G. and Den Hartog, H. (eds), Challenges for macroeconomic modelling, North-Holland, Amsterdam, 1988, pp. 389-399.

Papademos, L. and Modigliani, F. (1990), 'The supply of money and the control of nominal income', in Friedman, B.M. and Hahn, F.H. (eds), Handbook of Monetary Economics, vol 1, North-Holland, Amsterdam, pp. 399-494.

Papadia, F. (1983), 'Rationality of inflationary expectations in the European Economic Community Countries', Empirical Economics, 8, pp. 187-202.

Pearce, D.K. (1979), 'Comparing survey and rational measures of expected inflation', Journal of Money, Credit and Banking, 11, pp.447-456.

Pech, H (1994), 'The interest rate policy transmission process-the case of Austria', in BIS (1994), pp. 31-45.

Perilleux, V. and Wouters, R. (1994), 'The interest rate policy transmission process in Belgium', in BIS (1994), pp. 47-62.

Perron, P. (1989), 'The great crash, the oil price shock, and the unit root hypothesis', Econometrica, 57, pp. 1361-1401.

Pesando, J.E. (1975), 'A note on the rationality of the Livingston price expectations', Journal of Political Economy, 83, pp.849-858.

Pesaran, M.H. (1985), 'Formation of inflation expectations in British manufacturing industries', The Economic Journal, 95, pp. 948-975.

Pesaran, M.H. (1987), 'The limits to rational expectations', Basil Blackwell, Oxford.

Pesaran, M.H. and Wright, C.B. (1991), 'Using and assessing CBI data at the Bank of England', Bank of England Technical Paper no 37, Bank of England, London.

Phelps, E.S. (1967), 'Phillips curves, expectations of inflation, and optimal unemployment over time', Economica, 34, pp. 254-281.

Pigott, C. (1993), 'International interest rate convergence: a survey of the issues and evidence', Federal Reserve Bank of New York Quarterly Review, 18, pp. 24-37.

Pindyck, R.S. (1991), ' Irreversibility, uncertainty , and investment', Journal of Economic Literature, 29, pp. 1110-1148.

Poole, W. (1970), 'Optimal choice of monetary policy instruments in a simple stochastic macro model', Quarterly Journal of Economics, 84, pp. 197-216.

Poole, W. (1994), 'Monetary aggregate targeting in a low-inflation economy', in Fuhrer, J.C. (ed), 'Goals, Guidelines and Constraints facing Monetary Policymakers', Federal Reserve Bank of Boston Conference Series no 38, pp. 87-135.

Popper, H. (1990), 'International Capital Mobility: direct evidence from long-term currency swaps', International Finance Discussion Paper, 386, Board of Governors of the Federal Reserve System.

Popper, H. (1993), 'Long-term covered interest parity: evidence from currency swaps', Journal of International Money and Finance, 12, pp. 439-448.

Praetz, P.D. (1972), 'The distribution of share price changes', Journal of Business, 45, pp. 49-55.

Purvis, D.P. (1992), 'Monetary transmission mechanisms', in Newman, P., Milgate, M. and Eatwell, J. (eds), 'The New Palgrave Dictionary of Money and Finance', The Macmillan Press, London, pp. 763-765.

Ragnitz, J. (1994), 'Zinsstruktur und Wirtschaftswachstum', Kredit und Kapital, 27, pp. 11-29.

Robertson, D. (1992), 'Term Structure Forecasts of Inflation', The Economic Journal, 102, pp. 1083-1093.

Romer, C.D. (1996), 'Inflation and the growth rate of output', NBER Working Paper, no 5575, Cambridge (MA).

Romer, C.D. and Romer, D.H. (1996), 'Institutions for monetary stability', NBER Working Paper, no 5557, Cambridge (MA).

Roper, D.E. and Turnovsky, S.J. (1980),'Optimal exchange market intervention in a simple stochastic macro model', Canadian Journal of Economics, 13, pp. 296-309.

Sargent, T.J. (1976), 'A classical macroeconometric model for the United States', reprinted in Lucas, R.E. and Sargent, T.J. (eds), 'Rational expectations and econometric practice', George Allen and Unwin, London, pp. 521-553.

Sargent, T.J. (1979), 'Macroeconomic theory', Academic Press, Boston.

Sargent, T.J. and Wallace, N. (1975), 'Rational expectations, the optimal monetary instrument, and the optimal money supply rule', reprinted in Lucas, R.E. and Sargent, T.J. (eds), 'Rational expectations and econometric practice', George Allen and Unwin, London, pp. 215-229.

Sargent, T.J. and Wallace, N. (1976), 'Rational expectations and the theory of economic policy', reprinted in Lucas, R.E. and Sargent, T.J. (eds), 'Rational expectations and econometric practice', George Allen and Unwin, London, pp. 199-213.

Sauer, C. and Scheide, J. (1995), 'Money, Interest Rate Spreads and Economic Activity', Weltwirtschaftliches Archiv, 131, pp. 708-722.

Schich, S.T. (1996), 'Alternative Specifications of the German Term Structure and its Information Content regarding Inflation', Discussion Paper 8/96, Deutsche Bundesbank, Frankfurt a/M.

Scholing, E., and V. Timmerman, 1977, 'Länder und Branchenkonjunktur verbund' (Economic interdependence between countries and industries), Kyklos, 30, pp. 599-617 (in German).

Seitz, H. (1988), 'The estimation of inflation forecasts from business survey data', Applied Economics, 20, pp. 427-438.

Severn, A.K. (1983), 'Formation of Inflation expectations in the UK', European Economic Review, 20, pp. 349-363.

Shigehara, K. (1996), 'The options regarding the concept of a monetary policy strategy', in Deutsche Bundesbank (ed), 'Monetary policy strategies in Europe', Vahlen-Verlag, München, pp. 7-44.

Shiller, R.J. (1990), The Term Structure of Interest Rates', in 'Handbook of Monetary Economics', B.M. Friedman and F.H. Hahn, (eds), North-Holland, Amsterdam, pp. 627-715.

Sijben, J.J. (1977), 'Theoretische grondslagen van de monetaire politiek: een monetaristische visie', Maandschrift Economie, 42, pp.1-31 (in Dutch).

Sijben, J.J. (1992), 'Monetary policy in a game-theoretic framework', Jahrbücher für Nationalökonomie und Statistik, 210, pp. 233-253.

Sijben, J.J. (1994), 'Comments on the paper presented by Crockett (1994) (see above).

Sijben, J.J. (1995), 'Regels versus flexibiliteit in de monetaire politiek: Opnieuw bezien', Rotterdamse Monetaire Studies, vol 13 no 4, pp. 45-53.

Sijben, J.J. (1996), 'Banken en het gewijzigde intermediatieproces', Maandschrift Economie, 60, pp. 456-477 (in Dutch).

Simmons, P. and Weiserbs, D. (1992), 'Consumer price perceptions and expectations', Oxford Economic Papers, 44, pp. 35-50.

Sims, C.A. (1980), 'Macroeconomics and reality', Econometrica, 48, pp.1-48.

Sims, C.A. (1982), 'Policy analysis with econometric models', Brookings Papers on Economic Activity, 1, pp. 107-164.

Smeets, H.D., 1992, 'Stylized Facts zum Konjunkturverlauf in der Bundesrepublik Deutschland' (Stylized facts on German business cycles), Jahrbuch für Nationalökonomie und Statistik, 210, pp. 512-532 (in German).

Smets, F. (1995), 'Central bank macroeconometric models and the monetary policy transmission mechanism', in BIS (1995), pp. 225-267.

Smith, J. and McAleer, M. (1990), 'Alternative procedures for converting qualitative response data to quantitative expectations: an application to Australian manufacturing', Working Paper no 219, Department of Statistics, Australian National University.

Smith, P.E. (1972), 'Lags in the effect of monetary policy: a comment', The American Economic Review, 62, pp. 230-233.

Sobiechowski, D. (1996), 'Rational expectations in the foreign exchange market? Some survey evidence', Applied Economics, 28, pp. 1601-1611.

Stiglitz, J.E. and Weiss, A. (1981), 'Credit rationing in markets with imperfect information', The American Economic Review, 71, pp. 393-410.

Stock, J.H., 1987, 'Asymptotic Propertie of Least Squares Estimators of Cointegrating Vectors,' Econometrica, 55, pp. 1035-1056.

Stokman, A.C.J. (1991), 'Rentestructuur in Theorie en Empirie', Maandschrift Economie, 55, pp. 114-129.

Summers, L.H. (1991), 'How should long-run monetary policy be determined?', Journal of Money, Credit, and Banking, 23, pp. 625-631.

Svensson, L.E.O. (1994), 'Estimating and Interpreting Forward Interest Rates: Sweden 1992-1994', Working Paper no 4871, NBER, Cambridge (MA).

Svensson, L.E.O. (1994), 'Fixed exchange rates as a means to price stability: what have we learned?', European Economic Review, 38, pp. 447-468.

Svensson, L.E.O. (1996), 'Inflation forecast targeting: implementing and monitoring inflation targets', Working Paper, no 56, Bank of England.

Tanner, J.E. (1969), 'Lags in the effects of monetary policy: a statistical investigation', The American Economic Review, 59, pp. 794-805.

Tanner, J.E. (1972), 'Lags in the effects of monetary policy: reply and some further thoughts', The American Economic Review, 62, pp. 234-237.

Tanner, J.E. (1979), 'Are the lags in the effects of monetary policy variable?', Journal of Monetary Economics, 5, pp. 105-121.

Taylor, J.B. (1995), 'The monetary transmission mechanism: an empirical framework', Journal of Economic Perspectives, 9, pp. 11-27.

Taylor, J.B. (1996), 'How should monetary policy respond to shocks while maintaining long-run price stability-conceptual issues', in Federal Reserve Bank of Kansas City, 'Achieving Price Stability', pp. 181-197.

Theil, H. (1952), 'On the time shape of economic microvariables and the Munich Business Test', Review of the International Statistical Institute, 20, pp. 105-120.

Theil, H. (1958), 'Economic forecasts and policy', North-Holland, Amsterdam.

Thomas, D.G. (1995), 'Output expectations within manufacturing industry', Applied Economics, 27, pp. 403-408.

Throop, A.W. (1994), 'International financial market integration and linkages of national interest rates', Federal Reserve Bank of San Fransisco Economic Review, 3, pp. 3-18

Tobin, J. (1961), 'Monetary theory: new and old looks', The American Economic Review, 60, pp. 26-37.

Tobin, J. (1969), 'A general equilibrium approach to monetary theory', Journal of Money, Credit, and Banking, 1, pp. 15-29.

Tucker, D.P. (1966), 'Dynamic income adjustment to money supply changes', The American Economic Review, 56, pp. 433-449.

Turnovsky, S.J. (1970), 'Empirical evidence on the formation of price expectations', Journal of the American Statistical Association, 65, pp. 1441-1454.

Turnovsky, S.J. (1985), 'Short-Term and Long-Term Interest Rates in a Monetary Model of a Small Open Economy', Working Paper no 1716, NBER, Cambridge (MA).

Turnovsky, S.J. (1989), 'The Term Structure of Interest Rates and the Effects of Macroeconomic Policy', Journal of Money, Credit and Banking, 21, pp. 321-347.

Tzavalis, E. and Wickens, M.R. (1996), 'Forecasting inflation from the term structure', Journal of Empirical Finance, 3, pp. 103-122.

Van der Wal, D., 1991, 'Geloofwaardigheid van het Nederlandse wisselkoersbeleid' (The credibility of Netherlands exchange rate policy), Maandschrift Economie, 55, pp. 164-182.

Vasicek, O. (1977), 'An Equilibrium Characterization of the Term Structure', Journal of Financial Economics, 5, pp. 177-189.

Vining, D.R. and Elwertowski, T.C. (1976), 'The relationship between relative price and the general price level', American Economic Review, 66, pp. 699-708.

Visco, I. (1984), 'Price expectations in rising inflation', North-Holland, Amsterdam.

Walsh, C.E. (1993), 'Central bank strategies, credibility, and independence: a review essay', Journal of Monetary Economics, 32, pp. 287-302.

Waud, R.N. (1973), 'Proximate targets and monetary policy', Economic Journal, 83, pp. 1-20.

Waud, R.N. (1975), 'Information lags and the interest rate as a proximate monetary policy target', Oxford Bulletin of Economics and Statistics, 37, pp. 103-135.

Wellink, A.H.E.M. (1990), 'Mogelijkheden van het monetaire beleid na de liberalisering: de visie van de Nederlandsche Bank', Preadvies NIBE Jaardag 1990, pp. 5-45 (in Dutch).

Whitley, J. (1997), 'Economic models and policy-making', Bank of England Quarterly Bulletin, 37, pp. 163-173.

Woodford, M. (1994), 'Nonstandard indicators for monetary policy: can their usefulness be judged from forecasting regressions?', in Monetary Policy, Mankiw, N.G. (ed), Studies in Business Cycles, 29, NBER, Cambridge (MA).

Wu, Y. (1996), 'Are real exchange rates nonstationary? Evidence from a panel-data test', Journal of Money, Credit and Banking, 28, pp. 54-63.

Wu, Y. and Zhang, H. (1996), 'Mean reversion in interest rates: new evidence from a panel of OECD countries', Journal of Money, Credit and Banking, 28, pp. 604-621.

Young, P.C., 1992, 'On trend extraction models: comments on a paper by Garcia-Ferrer and Del Hoyo', Journal of Forecasting, 11, pp. 667-669.

Zarnowitz, V., 1991, 'What is a business cycle?' Working Paper Series no. 3863, NBER, Cambridge (Mass.)

Zarnowitz, V., 1992, 'Business Cycles: Theory, History and Forecasting', The University of Chicago Press, Chicago.

Index

Abel, 16
Abuaf, 50
Accountability, 14
Accuracy, 95, 97, 102, 123
Adjustment processes, 109,119
Akerlof, 3
A priori knowledge, 18
Arbitrage, 26, 40, 57, 122
ARIMA-models, 60, 61
Asymmetries in information, 8, 10, 29
Asymmetry parameter, 91, 93
Auerbach, 64
Availability of credit, 10

Balance sheet, 11, 12
Balcombe, 90
Ball, 6, 13
Bank of England, 11
Bank reserves, 9
Barrell, 13
Barro, 2, 87
Base drift, 3
Base money, 4
Basic component indicators, 60, 63-65, 67
Batchelor, 90, 91, 94, 98
Baumgartner, 18
Bean, 13
Bennink, 65
Berk, 66, 76
Bernanke, 2, 3, 5, 6, 8, 9, 34, 88, 96
Bernard, 25,33
Beveridge, 61
Bikker, 60,63, 65, 66, 75-77
BIS, Bank of International Settlements 7, 9, 10, 12
Blanchard, 14, 29
Blinder, 8, 9, 13, 15, 34
Bliss, 30
Blundell-Wignall, 45
Boschan, 63
Brandner, 61
Breeden, 27
Britton, 15
Brown, 45
Brunner, 3
Bryan, 15
Buiter, 19
Burger, 5
Burley, 65
Burns, 59
Business cycle, 20, 39, 59, 60, 63, 67, 121-123, 125
Business cycle duration, 61
Business cycle interrelationships, 60, 76, 77
Business International Corporation, 46, 47, 52, 57
Bry, 63

Campbell, 27, 30, 31, 48, 95
Carlson, 87, 90, 91, 102
Carlson-Parkin approach, 87, 89, 92
Canova, 61, 62
Case studies, 20, 124, 125, 126
Causality, 101, 102, 123, 124,
    In models, 60
    In VECM, 90, 100
Cavaglia, 46, 57
Census X-11, 60
Central bank liability, 4
Central Limit Theorem, 90
Cheung, 98
Chinn, 98
Christiano, 29
Christiansen, 45, 57
Classical dichotomy, 8
Clark, 61
Clinton, 32

Haldane, 10
Hall, 13, 18, 29
Hamilton, 18
Hardouvelis, 27, 30, 31, 32, 33, 67
Harvey, 32, 61, 62
Haubrich, 33
Heiner, 17
Henderson, 20
Henry, 18, 32
Hicks, 16
Hodrick-Prescott trend, 62
Hoogduin, 16, 17
Howrey, 17
Hu, 27, 32
Huang, 98
Hubbard, 15
Hysteresis, 14

Income effect, 12
Identification problems, 26
Identifying restrictions, 19
Independent central bank, 2
Indicator variables, see information variables
Inflation, 1, 3, 8, 20, 87, 109, 110, 119, 124, 125
  Costs of, 2
  Expectations, 5, 21, 28, 35, 87, 101,121, 123, 124
  Information content of expectations, 96, 99
  Inflation rate differentials, 109, 111
  Target, 3
Inflationary bias, 2
Information imperfections, 9
Information variable procedure, 23, 37
Information variables, 5,6 ,23, 24, 34, 36, 87, 101, 123
Ingersoll, 27
Inherent uncertainty, 17
Instruments, 1, 4, 7, 15, 19, 23, 121
Integration, 110-112, 115, 118, 120
Interaction economic agents and policy maker, 7
Interdependency inflation and growth, 25, 29
Interest rate targeting, 123
Intermediate target variables, 4-6, 23, 24, 34, 36, 87, 101
International interdependencies, 20, 121-123, 125
ISLM model, 28

Jackman, 13
James, 13
Johansen, 97
Johansens cointegration test, 97
Jondeau, 27, 31
Jorion, 31, 50

Kahn, 2
Kashyap, 10, 18
Kendall, 90
Keynes, 16
Keynesian theory, 8
Klein, 59, 66
Kloek, 65
Knightian risk, 16
Knightian uncertainty, see fundamental uncertainty
Koedijk, 25, 31
Kool, 25, 31
Koopmans, 64
Kuipers, 19
Kuismanen, 87
Kuttner 23
Kwiatkowski, 49
Kydland, 2, 14, 37, 87

Lahiri, 59
Layard, 13, 29
Leading indicators, 5, 59, 67, 123
Leck, van der, 16
Leeper, 19

Likelihood ratio tests, 97
Lindbeck, 29
Long and variable lags, 15-17, 23
Long term interest rate, 20, 39-41, 124
Lucas, 13, 16, 27, 35, 92
Lucas critique, 35, 37

MAPE, mean average prediction error, 94
Madsen, 88
Major swings in bond market, 41-42
Mankiw, 7, 8, 10, 13
Mauskopf, 9, 11
McAleer, 90, 104
McCallum, 34, 41, 52, 57
McKibbin, 20
Measurement without theory, 64
Measures of inflation expectations, 87
Meltzer, 3
Menon, 12
Menu costs, 13
Merton, 27
Mishkin, 2, 3, 5-7, 25-27, 30-33, 35-96
Mitchell, 59
Model, 113
Modigliani, 2, 3, 11, 20, 23, 26
Modigliani-Miller theorem, 9
Moersch, 32, 33
Monetary policy, 6, 17
Monetary strategy, 1, 6, 7, 17, 121
Monetary transmission mechanism, 7-14, 121, 123, 125, 126
    uncertainty and, 1, 14-19, 37, 45, 121,
Money neutrality, 8
Money stock, 5
Money targeting, 6, 23, 101
Moore, 59, 66
Moving average, 61, 81
Multi model approach, 15, 18, 121, 125, 126
Multiple unit roots, 96
Muth, 13,87

Naive forecasts, 95
NBER-method, 59
Nelson, 61
Neusser, 61
New classical theory, 8, 29, 32, 34
New keynesian theory, 8, 13, 27, 29, 34
Newey, 52
Ng, 61
Nickell, 13
Non-financial activity, 1, 3, 8, 10, 11, 14, 24, 33, 121
Non linearities, 93
Non stationarity, 48, 95
Normality test, 98

OECD, Organisation for Economic Cooperation and Development, 59, 61, 65, 66
Oliner, 10
Open market operations, 4, 10
Operational target, 4, 5, 6, 9
Orthogonality assumption, 62
Overnight rate, 4, 9

Palm, 8
Pantula, 96, 98
Papademos, 3, 20, 23
Papadia, 88, 98
Parkin, 87, 102
Pech, 12
Pesaran, 88, 90, 96, 103
Perceived inflation rate, 89, 92-93, 102
Perfect capital market, 10, 11, 45
Persistence of expected inflation rate, 95, 96, 102

Perilleux, 11
Perron, 48, 95, 112-116
Perry, 3
Perturbation, 111, 112, 114, 117, 124
Phase average trend, 63
Pigott, 45, 57
Policy maker, 4, 5, 15, 122, 124-126
Policy rules, 1, 6, 7, 23, 101
Policy targets, 1
Pindyck, 16
Polychotomous tendency surveys, 88, 89
Poole, 5, 6, 20, 23
Popper, 39, 57, 58
Praetz, 106
Prescott, 2, 37, 87
Price level, 2, 110, 111, 124
Price level target, 2
Price stability, 2, 3, 23, 87, 96, 109
Principal-agent problems, 10
Principal component analysis, 44, 65, 76-77
Priors, 19
Profitability, 109
Purvis, 9

Ragnitz, 32
Rational expectations, 13, 16 , 27, 31, 40, 57, 87
Rationality of inflation expectations, 96
Reaction function, see policy rule
Real business cycle theory, see new classical theory
Real interest rate, 26, 30, 31, 32, 34, 35
Recursive estimates, 118
Reference indices, 60, 63, 64, 66
Regime shifts, 35
Relative price, 111-114, 116, 117, 120
Reserve requirements, 4, 10
Response category, 92
Response function of consumers, 104
Response thresholds, 89, 92, 102, 104, 106
Ricart, 37, 31
Rigidity,
Nominal, 8, 13
Real, 8, 13
Real wage, 3
Risk, 26
Risk neutrality, 10, 45
Risk premium, 26, 27, 30, 45-47, 52, 57, 109, 122
RMSE, Root Mean Squared Error, 94
Robertson, 31
Romer, 3, 6-8, 10, 13
Roper, 20
Ross, 27
Rudebusch, 10
Rules versus discretion, 24

Sargent, 13
Sauer, 32
Scheide, 32
Schich, 31
Scholing, 66, 77, 79
Seasonal component, 60
Seitz, 90, 104
Shigehara, 14, 33
Shiller, 11, 27, 30, 31
Sijben, 2, 57, 11, 24, 101
Shortcuts vs overview, 19
Signal processing, 81, 92
Simmons, 88
Simulation experiments, 51, 116
Sims, 8, 19
Single monetary policy, 125
Skewness, 90
Smeets, 61
Smets, 25, 31, 35

Smith, 17, 90, 104
Smoothing procedure, 63
Snower, 29
Sobiechowski, 57
Sources of finance:
  Direct and intermediated, 11
  Internal and external, 10
Spillovers among markets, 43
Spolander, 87
Standing facilities, 41
Stein, 10, 18
Stiglitz, 8
Stock, 87
Stone, 87
Structural change, 112-117
Structural inflation rate, 112, 119, 120
Structural time series models, 61, 62, 81
Stuart, 90
Subjective conditional probability distribution, 89, 103
Substitution effect, 12
Summers, 3, 14
SUR-regression, 50, 54
Surveys, 6, 20, 87, 101, 122, 123, 124, 125
Survey-based measures of inflation expectations, 87
Sutch, 26
Svensson, 6, 12, 21, 87, 101
Swank, 19
Systematic forecast errors, 57

Tanner, 17
Taylor, 7, 39
Term premium: see risk premium
Term structure of interest rates; 11, 20, 23-26, 121, 122, 124, 125
  As a leading indicator, 32, 67
  Expectations theory of, 27, 30, 34
  Information content of, 24, 25, 28, 29, 31, 32
  General equilibrium models of, 27
  Monetary policy and, 33-35
  Preferred habitat theory of, 26
  Price adjustment and, 28, 29, 33, 36, 122
  Shocks and, 28, 33, 35, 36, 122
  Studies, 30-31
Testing the null of stationarity, 49
Theil, 90, 94
Time inconsistency, 2, 37
Timing, 64
Timmerman, 66, 77, 79
Tradeables, 114
Trade-off between price stability and economic growth, 3
Transmission mechanism, see Monetary transmission mechanism
Transparency, 1, 14
Trend, 60-62, 113-116, 119
Trend stationary, 110, 111, 113, 114, 117, 120
Tucker, 17
Turning point, 60, 63-65
Turnovsky, 20, 27, 34
Tzavalis, 26, 30

Ultimate target variables, 2, 3,5-7, 17, 20, 23, 36, 109, 111, 117, 119, 121
Unbiasedness assumption, 92, 98, 102
Uncertainty, 1, 15-17
UIP, Uncovered interest rate parity, 40, 45, 47, 52, 53, 57, 122, 123
Unferth, 44

Unit roots,
Multiple, 96
Panel data and, 150
Tests, 47, 48, 49, 95, 113
Unpredictability in behaviour, 16

Vasicek, 27
VAR, Vector autoregressive analysis, 18, 99, 101
VECM, Vector error correction model, 99
Verschoor, 46, 57
Vining, 90
Viñals, 2
Visco, 90, 103

Wage negotiations, 109, 116, 117
Wallace, 13
Walsh, 2
Waud, 17
Wealth effect, 12
Weiserbs, 88
Weiss, 8
Welfare, 2, 4
Wellink, 9, 12, 109
West, 52
White noise, 110
Whitley, 15, 17
Wickens, 26, 30
Wilcox, 10
Wolff, 46, 57
Woodford, 19, 102
World interest rate, 44
Wouters, 11
Wright, 90
Wu, 50

Yang, 98
Yield curve, see term structure
Young, 61, 62

Zarnowitz, 59, 61-63
Zero lower bound on interest rates, 3
Zha, 19
Zhang, 50
Z-score, 104

GPSR Compliance

The European Union's (EU) General Product Safety Regulation (GPSR) is a set of rules that requires consumer products to be safe and our obligations to ensure this.

If you have any concerns about our products, you can contact us on ProductSafety@springernature.com

In case Publisher is established outside the EU, the EU authorized representative is:

Springer Nature Customer Service Center GmbH
Europaplatz 3
69115 Heidelberg, Germany

Batch number: 10704043

Printed by Printforce, the Netherlands